The
CRAFT *of* GARDENS

Translated by Alison Hardie
Photographs by Zhong Ming

With a Foreword by Maggie Keswick

The
CRAFT of GARDENS

Ji Cheng

Better Link Press

Map of the Jiangnan region.

This book is edited and designed by the Editorial Committee of *Cultural China* series

Managing Directors: Wang Youbu, Xu Naiqing
Editorial Director: Wu Ying
Editors: Zhang Yicong, Yang Xiaohe

Text by Ji Cheng
Translated by Alison Hardie
Photographs by Zhong Ming
With a Foreword by Maggie Keswick

Cover Design by Wang Wei
Interior Design by Yuan Yinchang, Li Jing and Hu Bin

ISBN: 978-1-60220-008-1

Address any comments about *The Craft of Gardens* to:

Better Link Press
99 Park Ave
New York, NY 10016
USA

or

Shanghai Press and Publishing Development Company
F 7 Donghu Road, Shanghai, China (200031)
Email: comments_betterlinkpress@hotmail.com

Printed in China by Shenzhen Donnelley Printing Co., Ltd.

1 3 5 7 9 10 8 6 4 2

Title-page illustration: "Watercourses should be made firm with banks of stone." Ji Chang Yuan, Wuxi, Jiangsu province.

Endpapers: Wen Zhengming (1470 – 1559), *The Studio of True Appreciation,* 1557 (Shanghai Museum).

Contents

1 "It takes a long time to grow...trees old enough to give real shade." Note the harmony between the natural tree and the man-made wall, and the way the curve of the moon-gate echoes that of the tree trunk. Qing Teng Shuwu (Green Vine Study), Shaoxing. This was the home of the writer and artist Xu Wei (1521–1593). An eccentric character, he also acted as strategic adviser to Hu Zongxian, who was responsible for ending the attacks on the East China coast by Japanese pirates in the mid–sixteenth century. Xu Wei once went mad and was imprisoned for killing his wife, but he was later released.

CONTENTS

2 Wang Meng, *Retreat in the Qingbian Mountains* (Shanghai Museum). Wang Meng (1308 or 1301–1385) was, with Huang Gongwang, Ni Zan and Wu Zhen, known as one of the Four Great Masters of the Yuan dynasty. Here a scholar hermit's thatched dwelling is tucked away in the left middle distance amid an idealized landscape of mountains, trees and water, far from the disturbances of the everyday world.

Translator's Preface
To The Second Edition

I am very grateful to the Shanghai Press and Publishing Development Company for reissuing my translation of Ji Cheng's *Yuan Ye*. The book has been out of print for some years and, with growing Western interest in Chinese gardens, a number of would-be readers have been frustrated in their efforts to obtain a copy. I am delighted that it will now be available. Zhong Ming's beautiful photographs, both color and black-and-white, were a much admired feature of the original edition, capturing the feeling of Ji Cheng's garden aesthetic. In order to meet the expectations of a younger generation of readers and benefit from advances in printing technology, the illustrations have been updated with recent color photographs.

For this new edition I have made almost no changes to the text, apart from correcting some actual errors, particularly in the notes. It is over a quarter of a century since I rashly embarked on this translation, and if I were to do it now, I would do it very differently, so I decided that, rather than completely redoing it, it would be better to leave it as it was. One change I have made is to alter the transliteration of Ji Cheng's formal name (*zi*) from Wupi to Wufou; I am convinced by Cao Xun's argument for this pronunciation, which I was not aware of when I did the translation. My rendering of *Yuan Ye* (literally "garden smelting") as *The Craft of Gardens* has been criticized by some scholars as an under-translation; perhaps I should have had the courage to call it "The Garden Smith" originally, but I did not, so for better or worse it remains *The Craft of Gardens*.

My original "translator's preface" now seems to me extremely simplistic. It is possible now, and should have been possible even then, to give a much more nuanced account of Ji Cheng's social background (see Joseph McDermott's review of the original edition in *Garden History* 18 [1], 1990, pp.70–74; and Cao Xun, "Ji Cheng yanjiu," *Jianzhushi* [*The Architect*] 13 [1982], pp.1–16). I was wrong to say that the *Yuan Ye* fell into obscurity with the disgrace and death of Ji's patron Ruan Dacheng; the book is mentioned by Li Yu in the early Qing, and was evidently available on the market, as it was exported to Japan. Perhaps it eventually disappeared in China for no other reason than that it went out of fashion. Still, the association with Ruan Dacheng probably did Ji Cheng little good; we know very little of Ji compared to what we know about his contemporary (and probable rival) Zhang Lian, whose biography was written by various admirers associated with the political faction opposed to Ruan Dacheng. Indeed, there may have been a political element in the way that garden designers obtained their commissions, and even in the subtleties of garden design, but this is still an under-researched area.

The field of Chinese garden studies, both in China and in the West, has expanded enormously since *The Craft of Gardens* was first published in the early 1980's. For a survey of how it has developed, I refer readers to my introduction to the third edition of Maggie Keswick's *The Chinese Garden: History, Art and Architecture*. I would like to pay particular tribute to the work of Stanislaus Fung, who has studied the *Yuan Ye* in depth for many years and produced many brilliant insights into the nature of the text and the deployment of space which it represents.

When I first embarked on this translation I knew almost nothing about Chinese gardens or indeed the world of the late Ming. To complete the translation, I had to learn a lot—in particular, I could not have managed without the annotated edition by Chen Zhi (1899–1989), one of the masters of garden studies and former professor of Nanjing Forestry University, even though I did not always follow his interpretation—and I have continued to learn ever since. The subject has given me an enormous amount of interest and enjoyment, and has brought me into contact with many congenial and stimulating colleagues. I would like to dedicate this second edition of *The Craft of Gardens* to the memory of the late Maggie Keswick, as the originator and supporter of the project.

Alison Hardie
January 2011

TRANSLATOR'S PREFACE

Almost nothing is known of the life of Ji Cheng. He lived during the late sixteenth and early seventeenth centuries, in the last years of the Ming dynasty, at a time of great social change and political upheaval. He seems to have been of humble origins, and is not known to have written anything other than his great work on garden design, the *Yuan Ye* or *Craft of Gardens*. No garden known to have been designed by him still exists.

Although Ji Cheng describes himself as having traveled quite widely, it appears from what he himself says that most of his work was done in his native Jiangsu. This was (as it still is) an extremely prosperous part of China, and as such attracted many wealthy men of culture who wanted to live in an agreeable and comfortable environment, far from the pressures of life in the capital, and attracted also the artists and craftsmen who depended on their patronage. Many of the finest artists of the late Ming were natives of the Jiangsu region, often from wealthy landowning families; possibly the greatest of these artists, Dong Qichang (1555–1636), was a friend of one of Ji Cheng's patrons, Zheng Yuanxun.

The late Ming was a time of social and economic change when the emergence of a wealthy merchant class with aspirations to join the cultured upper class created a strong demand for manuals of self-improvement and advice on what was and was not socially acceptable. *The Craft of Gardens* evidently belongs to some extent in this genre, since a member of the old-established literati would hardly feel a need for Ji Cheng's advice on, for example, which type of balustrade design was vulgar and which was elegant. Ji Cheng himself seems to be an example of someone who, in the comparative social mobility of the time, made his name through his skills, without any advantage of birth.

The Craft of Gardens, written between 1631 and 1634, is the first surviving—and possibly actually the first—general manual on landscape gardening in the Chinese tradition. It is very unlike what a westerner would expect of a gardening manual, since it rarely mentions any particular plant by name and gives almost no advice on how to grow anything. By contrast, it pays close attention to architecture, an inseparable part of the Chinese concept of garden design, and to the selection of various kinds of rocks to form part of the landscape.

Ji Cheng's method of "teaching" garden design is not to give step-by-step instructions, which would in any case be unrealistic when dealing with something as individual as a piece of landscape, though on some matters, such as the construction of various types of window, he goes into considerable detail. Instead he emphasizes the importance of basing the garden design on the existing nature and features of the landscape, and uses poetic descriptions to build up an atmosphere which will inspire the would-be designer to create a garden which can express the emotions he is experiencing.

Despite its originality, Ji Cheng's work fell into obscurity for several centuries. The main reason for this was that one of his most important patrons, Ruan Dacheng, who wrote a preface for the book and arranged for its publication, was a political associate of the notorious court eunuch Wei Zhongxian, who contributed substantially to the decline and fall of the Ming dynasty. Not only was Ruan Dacheng associated with Wei Zhongxian, he also voluntarily surrendered to the Manchu invaders who established the Qing dynasty. The odium which these actions brought on Ruan's associates meant that Ji Cheng's book virtually disappeared. It was rediscovered by Japanese scholars of garden design only in the early part of the present century, and was reprinted in China for the first time in 1931, almost exactly three hundred years after its original publication.

The language of the book is a curious combination of a highly mannered literary style, reminiscent of Silver Latin, with down-to-earth practical language appropriate to a do-it-yourself manual and incorporating a certain amount of Ji Cheng's native Jiangsu dialect. Chinese scholars have found that some of the technical terms used by Ji Cheng in relation to architecture are still used by craftsmen in Suzhou. The contrast between the two styles is so sharp that Professor Chen Congzhou (1918–2000) of Tongji University, who is one of the great modern authorities on Chinese gardens, suspects that Ji Cheng, as an uneducated man distrustful of his own literary ability, may have commissioned a ghost-writer for the poetic sections. Certainly it would not have been difficult to find some down-at-heel scholar in Ruan Dacheng's household who would have been glad to do the job.

To a modern reader, the real attraction of *The Craft of Gardens* lies in its plainer passages, where Ji Cheng speaks directly to his readers. He comes across as a strong and individual personality, proud of his success as a creative artist and of having risen out of the artisan class, practical, unpretentious, and with the ability to visualize every garden as a complex and complete entity. His views on garden design deserve to be known to a wider readership, and if this translation does anything to help people either to express some of the ideas behind Chinese landscape gardening in their own gardens, or to learn a little more about the whole network of concepts which underlies Chinese culture as a whole, I shall be more than satisfied.

For this translation, I have used a modern (1978) edition of *The Craft of Gardens* (*Yuan Ye Zhu Shi*) edited by Professor Chen Zhi, with contributions by Yang Chaobo and Chen Congzhou. This edition is based on the text published in 1931 by the Chinese Architectural Society (Zhongguo Yingzao Xueshe). I should like to express my indebtedness to Professor Chen Zhi's notes and translation into modern Chinese, which were of inestimable value to my understanding of the original text. All translations in my notes are by me unless otherwise stated. In my version I have added the headings "Structural Features" and "Scenic Features" to make the arrangement of the

3 (facing page) Sites among mountain forests: "Terraces will rise at varying heights...." Hu Pao Si, Hangzhou. The Hu Pao Si or Running Tiger Temple is a temple complex founded in the Tang dynasty and built around the Running Tiger Spring near the city of Hangzhou in Zhejiang province.

various sections more consistent. Otherwise I have tried to follow the original text exactly. The diagrams in the main text are all from the original book and the captions to them are Ji Cheng's own. Captions to the plates are mine.

In the translation and notes I have used the standard hanyu pinyin transliteration for Chinese words and names, except where there is a very well-established rendering in English, such as Confucius. The main thing to remember about hanyu pinyin is that "c" represents a sound like "ts," "q" represents "ch," and "x" represents "hs."

This is perhaps also the place for a note on the oddities of Chinese nomenclature. Members of the educated classes would be known by their original family surname and a personal name (the latter was given when they started going to school; before that they would be known by a "milk-name" or baby name); in addition they would, as adults, take a more formal literary name by which they would be known to less intimate friends and associates. Most literary men would also have one or several additional titles which they would either choose themselves or otherwise acquire (such as the painter Huang Gongwang's pen-name "The Daoist of Great Folly" or the poet Tao Yuanming's official title "Warden Tao"). Thus our author's family name is Ji and his personal name Cheng; but his patrons Zheng Yuanxun and Ruan Dacheng refer to him by his formal name of Ji Wufou or simply Wufou. At the end of his Author's Foreword, Ji Cheng signs himself by his pen-name, "The Negative Daoist."

Finally, I should like to express my gratitude to the following people: my parents for having instinctively created gardens in the spirit of Ji Cheng and for having passed on to me something of their feeling for natural gardens; Maggie Keswick for initiating the whole project and contributing the Foreword; Zhong Ming for his photography, for general support and encouragement and for being a living exemplar of the traditional literatus; Margaret Hardie for patiently typing my original manuscript; Dick Hall and Christine Moore for making available the resources of their library; Professor Chen Congzhou of Tongji University for advice given in person and inspiration given through his books; Professor Shih Hsio-yen and Ms Dimon Liu of Hong Kong University for help and advice; and other friends whose encouragement, practical help and patience in listening to me have been invaluable. The faults and inadequacies of my translation and notes are of course my sole responsibility.

A. M. H.
London–Hong Kong

FOREWORD *by Maggie Keswick*

The gardens with which this book is concerned are among the loveliest in the world. In essence they are secret gardens, enclosed, even in country sites, by walls or wattle fences that reveal only the tips of their pavilions and trees to the world outside. Within they are just as hidden: walls enclose walls, and courtyards, still smaller courtyards, until the whole garden becomes a refined and complex maze which unfolds itself only when, lured on by glimpses of further delights just beyond the next enclosure, the visitor makes his way gently along its zigzag paths.

The earliest description of such a garden comes in a poem from the *Songs of Chu*, a collection from one of the southern kingdoms that flourished in the fourth century BC along the Yangtze valley. In it a shaman singer describes the king's palace, where lattice-work doors open onto galleries murmurous with the sounds of gullies and streams. Vermilion balustrades lean out to catch the scent of lotus which has just opened in the serpentine pool below. Above, high, stepped terraces and "storied pavilions" open views to the distant hills. Two thousand years on, this could still be a garden in China. But, although descriptions by their owners and historians have preserved the fame of many gardens down the centuries, when Ji Cheng laid out inkstone and brush in 1631 to record his experience as a landscape gardener, he was, as far as anyone knows, the first Chinese ever to do so.

He wears the weight of a two-thousand-year-old tradition lightly. Conventions are assessed and discarded if they do not make sense: "Why insist on keeping a corridor at the rear, looking as if it were tacked on superfluously?" And why set up a pavilion on top of rocks if there is no view from it? Even important recommendations by the *fengshui* geomancer—who the Chinese believed could alter family fortunes by the favorable placing of buildings and graves—need not be slavishly followed. Ji Cheng's experience makes him practical—elaborate wall-carving is absurd in gardens since birds soon mess it up with nests—but also finely tuned to aesthetic bathos, so that, for example, small and ill-made artificial mountains are written of as "decorations in a gold-fish bowl."

Ji Cheng lived at a time of social upheaval. He made gardens not in the time-sanctified manner of a gentleman amateur, but professionally, for private clients as likely to be newly successful silk or salt merchants as the retired government officials of the past. Just as, today, rising New Yorkers seeking social acceptance buy "art" to show they are both up-to-date and cultured, or the English, eager to imply their riches have been established over generations, use new wealth to buy old country houses, so, along the Yangtze valley, the *nouveaux riches* of the late Ming built gardens to show they could be as cultivated as the scholars of the mandarinate. Behind Ji Cheng's judgements one may just hear the echoes of their ill-conceived requests (for carved walls? for goldfish-bowl mountains?). He sweeps these away in a convenient catch-all that puts him in control: "a garden must be in accordance with the spirit of the times"—and then promises the ultimate success—"while [it] elicits the appreciation of the most cultivated visitors."

The Appreciation of Nature

Like Ji Cheng, what these cultivated visitors would have appreciated above all was a garden that made them feel in tune with nature. In China appreciation of nature is very ancient. A poet of the fifth century BC is filled with terror as he describes the peaks and chasms of a mountain journey, holding them in numinous awe. In Europe such wild landscapes represented the chaos from which Christianity would rescue man's immortal soul: not until the fifteenth century did Petrarch become the first European to climb, for pleasure, the mountains near his Vaucluse home, and he found himself torn by guilt lest the beauty he experienced should entice him away from God. By that time, the Chinese, unhindered by a concept of the soul, had been in love with the beauty of untamed nature for more than ten centuries. Indeed, mountains had themselves become inextricably linked with spirituality.

In the third century, seven sages of the Bamboo Grove sat among the hills discussing the finer points of esoteric Daoism. When vulgarians approached them with worldly talk, they rolled their eyes up into their heads and waited for them to depart. One of the sages, Liu Ling, sat naked in his hut; when visitors complained of this, he answered: "I take the whole world as my house and my own room as my clothing. Why then do you enter here, into my trousers?" His trousers, house and the universe were interchangeable: he had achieved the Daoist ideal, unity with all things.

In fact, not only Daoists, but all the Chinese philosophical schools held that everything in existence is composed of the same fundamental *qi* or breath. It is an idea that would become immensely important to landscape painting and through it, as we shall see, to the making of gardens. When *qi* is pure and light it rises to become heaven, when muddy and heavy it falls to form the earth. But the breath that blends both becomes man, who thus stands midway, united by this essence with everything else that exists. Contemplation of nature triggers this latent sense of unity: a man who stands in the spring snow gazing intensely into a cloud of plum blossom may suddenly feel his heart unfold, as if it too were flowering, as vigorously and spontaneously as the tiny twigs themselves. In this way he experiences, through nature, the mysterious working of the *Dao*.

The other philosophical schools also used the word *dao*, in its original meaning of "the way," but Daoists appropriated it to stand for the ultimate "totality of all things"—past, present and future—in its state of continuous transformation and change. Like a vast, seamless web of all creation, the swirling patterns of the *Dao* form and dissolve quickly, as in the patterns of clouds, or slowly over aeons of time, like the earth itself. Yet in a larger sense it never changes, for the sum of its forces is always the same.

Through breathing exercises, diet and sexual techniques, Daoist adepts aimed so to refine their material bodies that they became one with these eternal currents. For those who were successful, death would become just another transformation—no more than the sleep of a butterfly. However, to delay this inevitable event a little, the Daoists also began to seek an elixir of life and to search in the mountains for the magic mushrooms of immortality. And they found that this wandering itself helped to distance them from the inconsequential cares of men, the better to sense the rhythms of the *Dao*.

Buddhism, which gradually infiltrated into China from India from the first century, later also made use of this indigenous idea. Monasteries were sited—as we see them in a thousand landscape paintings—high in the hills, their upturned roofs echoing the swoops and hollows of the crags around them; below, the soundless, misty depths of valleys became symbols of the Void. Monastery gardens preserved trees that survived to a remarkable age—something impossible elsewhere in a country starved of fuel. And Buddhist laymen also sometimes sought retreat from the "World's dust" (to use a Chinese phrase) in country estates. The most famous of these, lying along the Wang River some thirty miles north of the Tang capital at Chang'an, was made by Wang Wei (701?–761), an artist, calligrapher, musician and poet. The scroll painting and poems he made of his Wang Chuan Villa were endlessly copied and recopied down the years, not only because of the physical charm of the villa's gentle hills and pavilions, nor even because of delicacy and brilliance of the scroll itself, but because the character of the man who made it imbued the garden—and his painting—with a profound and tranquil feeling of erudition and spirituality. In the words of the modern historian Wango Weng, this is what "every Chinese scholar since would like to recreate around him."

4 Copy by an anonymous Song dynasty artist of Wang Wei's painting of the Wangchuan estate (National Museum of China). Wang Wei's original painting of his own estate no longer survives and is known only through later copies such as this, which vary between themselves but may give some idea of the original composition.

Already by the third century "longing for mountains and waters" had become synonymous with the life of the spirit. One great official, asked his opinion of a new Prime Minister, replied: "in official matters I am no better, but in appreciation of hills and waters I think I surpass him." Meanwhile Tao Yuanming (365 or 372 or 376–427) became the first great poet to crystallize this emotion, and to give lyric form to the ideal of a cultivated scholar's retreat. At first he obeyed the promptings of his family and, unwillingly accepting an official appointment, fell into the "web of the World's dust." Years later, released back "to Nature and to Freedom," he returned to a patch of the southern moor he had rescued from the wilderness:

> I lean on the south window and let my pride expand
> I consider how easy it is to be content with a small space,
> Every day I stroll in the garden for pleasure…
> As the sun's rays grow dim and disappear from view,
> I walk round my lonely pine tree, stroking it.

When over a thousand years later Ji Cheng claims that his gardens will "fully satisfy your craving for woods and spring," he is still implying (although by now it is hardly more than a convention) not just a physical or emotional need, but a spiritual one.

The Confucian Aspect

In China, however, it was not always easy to take off for the mountains, abandoning family and friends and civic duties. Buddhists might wish to remove themselves from earthly desires, while the Daoist Lao Zi had shown a way for man to fit into the great universe in which he lived. But his contemporary, Confucius, was meanwhile speaking equally powerfully of how he was to live harmoniously amongst his fellow men. Daoists believed in *wu wei*, "no action contrary to nature," but Confucians, in the rites and duties of a well-organized society. In particular, Confucius emphasized the necessity for an ethical man to render service to the state, and, in the Han dynasty (206 BC–220 AD) his teachings, somewhat adapted, became state orthodoxy. For approximately the next two thousand years stringent imperial examinations in the Confucian classics weeded out the unworthy and filled civil-service posts across the land with a highly cultivated and extensively educated elite (a considerable achievement, if one compares this elite, say, with the generally brutish and ignorant barons of Europe in the Middle Ages).

As concerns the history of gardens, it is important to understand that, in traditional China, a position in the mandarinate was the only acceptable route to wealth and prestige, so that families exerted the greatest pressure on their sons to be successful candidates. A man of promise who endangered his person and prospects by taking to the hills was unlikely to be commended for filial piety; once in office, it was not easy to escape. The solution lay in recreating nature more accessibly in gardens. The pavilions and garden-rooms of those well sited in the countryside could provide summer accommodation within an acceptable distance of civilization, while preserving the illusion of escape. However, as one scholar-official remarked, "if the heart is at peace, why should one not create a wilderness even in the midst of town?" All that was needed was a high wall to exclude the cares of men, and then the inside could be returned to nature. Here, in the company of a few like-minded friends and a jar of wine, the harassed official could assuage his longing for mountains and waters while still fulfilling his duties to the state and his family. In fact his family might even enjoy it too.

The example of the Buddhist Vimalakirti helped in this. As a householder who yet managed to achieve Buddhahood by "remaining unmoved in the midst of movement," he reinforced the Confucian tradition (so unlike that of Europe's celibate priests) of a married elite—whose gardens were thus used for family parties as well as for contemplation.

In particular, gardens came to be used as settings for artistic endeavor. Confucius had spent most of his life out of office, and his ethics included an ideal of self-cultivation and relaxation through the arts, both to replenish an official's energy and to make best use of his time when unemployed. Gardens became an acceptable venue for writing poetry, practicing calligraphy or admiring antiques, and the French phrase *cultiver son jardin* has added meaning in China. In the Song dynasty, when a political faction led by Sima Guang was ousted at court, this great official retired to his garden in the middle of Luoyang and there, in his library surrounded by *wutong* trees, wrote one of China's greatest histories. In between chapters he trimmed his herbs, fished in his little stream and, by tying together their leafy tips, made a living tent from tree bamboos he had planted in a ring. It has long ceased to exist, but Sima Guang's tender descriptions of this "Garden for Solitary Enjoyment," or Du Le Yuan, have made it, with Wang Wei's villa, one of the best-loved historical gardens in China.

Many gardens were open to visitors on festivals and holidays, and a well-known literary work of the Song, the *Luoyang Ming Yuan Ji,* describes eighteen famous gardens in Luoyang at a time that is often nostalgically seen as the golden age of all the arts, including gardens. In Ji Cheng's home province of Jiangsu, especially in the cities of Jiangnan, south of the Yangtze River, there remain a number of old gardens which, though much altered over time, can still take us back to his era—and even before. One, called the Tui Si Yuan (Retreat to Think Garden), still exists in Tongli, Ji Cheng's hometown, and contains the Tui Si Cao Tang which has been described as one of the most beautiful pavilion buildings in China. It dates, however, only from 1865. The most famous older gardens are in Suzhou, set off narrow lanes, tucked in among the canals and plane-lined streets and double-storied courtyard houses of this old and cultivated city. Among them is the Cang Lang Ting, or Pavilion of the Blue Waves, in which is preserved a stone-etched plan of how it looked in 1044. Perhaps because of this, it retains an almost identical layout today. Private gardens also continued to flourish under the following Yuan dynasty, because old families loyal to the conquered Song refused to participate in the new Mongol government. In Suzhou another garden begun at this time can still be visited: it is the Shi Zi Lin or Stone Lion Grove, first made by the Yuan painter Ni Zan, though in this case irretrievably altered from the drawing he left of it and from the spare and elegant style which was the hallmark of his art.

By the time the Ming dynasty returned a Chinese emperor to the throne

5 Mountains and water, He Yuan, Yangzhou, Jiangsu. The He Yuan or He Family Garden—of which the garden section is known as the Jixiao Shanzhuang (Resounding Roars Mountain Villa)—is the largest surviving example in Yangzhou of what was originally a private garden residence. It was built in the late nineteenth-early twentieth century for He Zhidao, a wealthy official of the imperial salt monopoly.

in 1368, the Confucian ideal of the retired scholar-without-portfolio was well accepted. And, since the Ming was a repressive and autocratic dynasty, it reinforced the option for a gentleman to reject public office and devote his time to the advancement of his spiritual, literary and artistic gifts in the elegant setting of a garden. The great Ming artist Wen Zhengming (1470–1559), who partly designed the Zhuo Zheng Yuan, or Garden of the Unsuccessful Politician, in Suzhou, made only one brief and unsatisfactory excursion into public employment and then, calling himself always an amateur, he lived for a time among the watery mazes of this lovely place, devoting himself to poetry and painting. During the same dynasty, Ji Cheng, the professional, began work on his treatise, laying the foundations of natural spontaneity and cultivated taste on which, it was unofficially agreed, good garden design must rest. In particular, he emphasized "appropriateness" and "suitability," matching the style of the garden to the existing features and atmosphere of a site in a way that anticipates Alexander Pope's advice, in eighteenth-century England, that a gardener must consult the "genius of the place" in all.

On Being Natural with Nature

Ji Cheng's reputation as garden-maker began (he tells us in his Preface) with amused disbelief in the rockery "mountains" he saw piled up in gardens near his home. He set out to do better, arranging earth and rocks together so that they resembled naturally formed rocky outcrops. We may surmise that, in the

hands of less talented men than Wen Zhengming, the tradition of garden-making when Ji Cheng came to it had grown somewhat ossified and artificial. Professional families of "false mountain" master-craftsmen followed long-established aesthetic and technical conventions and measured their success against other artificially constructed rockeries. By looking again at natural rock formations, Ji Cheng revitalized the whole approach, developed new engineering methods and inspired admiration in those who saw his work. He did not, however, alter at all the Chinese idea of what a garden should be. His is the summation of a tradition, a subtle reinvigoration of long-accepted conventions, not a revolution, and he takes for granted that his reader will be as familiar with his basic assumptions about garden-making as he is.

To those seeing them for the first time, however, the Chinese conviction that their gardens are "natural" (especially as opposed to the "artificial" gardens of Japan) may come as something of a surprise. Firstly there are the rocks. Huge single rocks are set up, much as sculpture is in western gardens, sometimes alone on plinths, sometimes in a group with smaller rocks and shrubs. Like nature's answers to Henry Moore, they rise from their narrowest points, both muscular and delicate, their sides swooping in curves and hollows, pitted with fissures and holes, miracles of balance and strength. There are also the "false mountains," *jia shan*, of Chinese gardens: huge piles of pitted rock held together by invisible wires, cement and the garden-maker's competence in dynamic equilibrium. Often they seem to dominate the garden, looming twelve feet high into the courtyards, running wild along the shores of pools and small lakes. Sometimes they are hollowed into caves

6 Group of buildings, Ge Yuan (Isolated Garden), Yangzhou, Jiangsu. The Ge Yuan was built in the late eighteenth to early nineteenth centuries for a wealthy salt merchant, Huang Yingtai, on the site of an older garden, the Garden of the Herb of Long Life, which was supposedly designed by the great and eccentric late Ming-early Qing painter, Shi Tao (1641–c.1718). The Ge Yuan is particularly famous for its bamboo and its "mountains," and is a very fine example of the garden designer's art. Clear Ripples Pavilion is to the right; the building in the background is called "Spring Comes naturally to the Paradise within the Flask" (Hu Tian Zi Chun) (see note 104).

7 Covered walkway, Zhan Yuan (Outlook Garden), Nanjing, Jiangsu. This garden originates from the early Ming dynasty (fourteenth century); it was given its present name in the eighteenth century by the Qianlong emperor, who stayed here on a tour of inspection. Some of the rocks in the garden are said to be left-overs from the Patterned Rock Convoy (see note 162).

for summer shade, sometimes planted with trees and smoothed with earthy banks, and sometimes they are labyrinths of little paths and steps leading up to a belvedere. Not just the feet, but the visitor's eyes move restlessly over these fragmented shapes, seeking a place to pause.

In the Chinese scheme of things such rocks, combined with streams and pools, form the basis of a garden's plan. The Chinese word for landscape, *shan shui*, means literally "mountains and waters," while a common phrase for making a garden, again translated literally, is "digging ponds and piling mountains." In nature, mountains form the skeleton of the earth, streams its arteries; in a garden, rocks form the bony structure, water, its living pulse. The rocks are hard, unmoving, powerful—the "masculine", *yang* element which must harmonize with the reflective, flowing *yin* of water. It is a juxtaposition of polar opposites that the Chinese, from very ancient times, have seen as the moving principle of the universe—*yin* forever giving way to *yang*, and *yang* to *yin*, in the unceasing motion of a pendulum.

On finding these two elements pleasingly balanced in a natural site, the Chinese, at least from the time of the Seven Sages, also felt an urge to embellish them with some small tokens of man. Placed in the hills or by lakes, little roofed and open-sided pavilions transform whole landscapes into *jardins trouvés*: views of them focus the wilderness; views from them are framed in their pillars. "Once we have a *ting*," one saying goes, "we can say we have a garden."

In the garden, too, pavilions overlook pools and are set on rocky hills. However, in nature they are tiny in proportion to the whole; in the garden

8 "Precipitous mountain." Wang Shi Yuan, Suzhou, Jiangsu. The rockery structure rising out of the water contrasts with the flat white wall and the straight lines of the pavilion columns.

they are only one among a huge variety of building types: two-storied *lou* or *ge*; little gazebos built near water *(xie)*; formal halls *(tang)*; summer-houses shaped like boats *(fang)*; small, linear belvederes *(xuan)*; poetry and painting studios; and libraries (without which no garden can be considered seriously). Smaller halls, covered porches to rest in, bridges, walls enlivened with grill-work windows and circular moongates—all these and more come pressing in on the garden visitor, close-packed in almost bewildering succession as he walks, and turns, and doubles back, and turns again along the pebble-paved paths and open galleries that define his route. The buildings are bowered in trees and bamboo groves whose shadows move against the lime-washed walls. Planting softens the edges of terraces and layers longer views with drifts of blossom, leaves and scent. But while the English speak of "planting" a garden, the Chinese "build" one: an educated Chinese gentleman visiting Europe in the 1920s commented in amazement on a "mown and bordered lawn which, while no doubt of interest to a cow, offers nothing to the intellect of a human being." For the British, long settled on peaceful, damp and temperate islands, rolling swards of cropped green grass are soothing and restful to the eye. Behind each suburban patch lies a dream of country parkland, the wealth of acres. But the Chinese are rice-growers, and pastureland can suggest only, however faintly across the centuries, nomadic cattle-raiders—barbarians beyond the benefits of civilization—riding south to plunder Chinese settlements. And what have such plunderers to do with cultivation, either of plants or the minds of men?

Clearly what seems "natural" to one culture can be strangely upsetting to another. And to understand how the Chinese came so strongly to defend the "naturalness" of their gardens one needs to know how it was these gardens came to look the way they do—and that involves something of their history, of magic and, above all, of painting.

The Immortals in the Garden

Hieroglyphs on tortoise shells and oracle bones from the second millennium BC refer to vast tracts of land set aside for the hunting parks and military maneuvers of China's ancient kings. Under Qin Shi Huang Di, the ruler who first unified all the Chinese kingdoms in 221 BC (and who was buried near modern Xi'an with the famous terracotta army to defend him in death), these ancient hunting enclosures began to take on a new significance. Around his capital he replicated the palaces of the conquered kings and, in the great Shang-lin park north of the city, collected animals and vegetation as tribute from all corners of his new-made empire. Thus he showed himself master of all he ruled.

The Han rulers who came after Qin Shi Huang knew a potent symbol when they saw one. Unlike conquerors before them, they retained the parks of their predecessor, added to them and set the great prose-poets of their time to record them. It is in the fantastic descriptions of these poems, in which magic and reality fuse to create a mythic portrait of the empire in miniature, that there is the first flowering of the idea that a garden is more than just the pleasing adornment of a particular piece of nature. Instead it becomes a microcosm, symbolizing all the riches, variety and beauty of the earth. It is an idea that, in the concentration of effects, even in small spaces, still influences gardens in China today.

It was the Han emperor Wudi who first gave form to another theme that makes Chinese gardens unlike any others. Wudi was much concerned with mortality. Before him, Qin Shi Huang had sent an expedition to the Eastern Seas to find the magic isles of the Chinese Immortals, mythical beings who, having extended their mortal span by a few hundred years, could vanish and appear with the wind or fly about on the backs of storks. They lived either in mountain palaces with the Queen Mother of the West, or on rocky islands in the Eastern Seas which, as Qin Shi Huang's expedition had approached them, dissolved into mist. Instead of trying to go to them, therefore, Wudi determined to bring the Immortals to him. And, to lure them down as they flew by on their storks, he ordered an enormous lake and three islands to be built in his hunting park. The islands were to be embellished with trees, blossom and animals so exotic and beautiful that the Immortals would confuse them with their own and, descending, would in gratitude tell the emperor their secret. Although the Immortals never appeared and Wudi died in normal old age, he achieved a different kind of immortality, for the fame of his park and its islands set a pattern for gardens that was to find expression not only on the Chinese mainland, but in the lakes and stone islets of

Japanese gardens too.

Today Chinese rockeries still bring a kind of magical strangeness into the garden. Their contorted shapes and towering peaks, reflected in the luminous smoothness of their complementary lakes, are meant to be slightly alienating—a contrast to the delicate prettiness of willows and swoop-eaved summer-houses. Wandering in these rockeries when the guides and visitors have gone, it is not too difficult to imagine an Immortal, bent with age but with skin as smooth as a baby's, materializing in the dusk.

Painting and Gardens

Ideas of the garden as a microcosm and as the haunt of the Immortals go some way towards elucidating the *magical naturalism* of gardens whose appeal, aided by myth and history, is not only to the senses but to the mind. In particular, however, it is impossible to see a garden through Chinese eyes without having some appreciation of Chinese landscape painting.

"The question of reality will not really bother [the visitor]," says a twentieth-century Chinese, "as soon as he ceases to be in the *garden* and starts to live in the *painting*." Almost all garden-makers were also painters, including Ji Cheng, whose secret in mountain-building is not only to take into account natural rock formations, but to "follow cracks… imitating the brushwork of the old masters," linking the fissured boulders into a sculptured whole. By a combination of skill and the mellowing passage of time, "it need not be obvious that a mountain is artificial…," for "the buildings and terraces will grow to look like a painting." Artificiality is no longer the antithesis of reality, but of art.

When Ji Cheng and his patrons looked at real mountains they saw them through eyes educated by a thousand years of landscape painting. When they arranged rocks and bamboo and their shifting shadows against a whitewashed wall, the wall became the equivalent of empty silk, the background of a landscape scroll. In certain lights—at dawn or dusk, or sometimes in the blinding glare of summer noon—the wall might even seem to have melted away altogether, leaving the rocks and bamboo floating

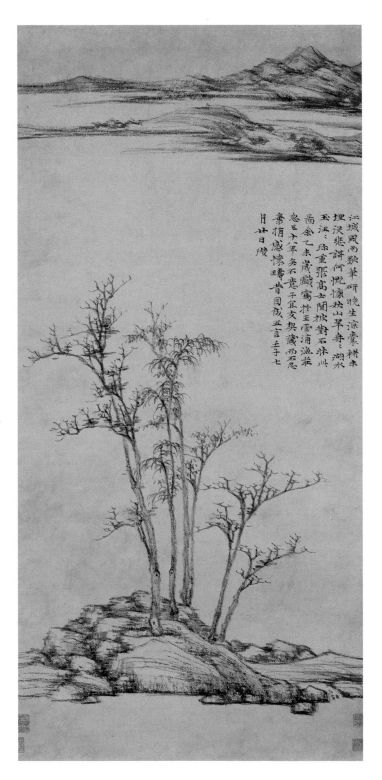

9 Ni Zan, the Master of the Cloud Forest (1306 or 1301-1374), *Fishing Village on a Clear Autumn Day*, 1356 (Shanghai Museum). This is an example of the simplicity and spaciousness aimed at in garden design as much as in landscape painting.

in the horizonless and vaporous distances of a painting by Ni Zan. Shrinking himself in imagination to the size of an ant, the connoisseur could wander in these misty wastes among rocks now grown into mountains, and shrubs and grasses as big as trees and forests. And as he walked and paused, the landscape unfolded around him as if he were taking a three-dimensional stroll through one of his own paintings, slowly unrolling the horizontal scroll from right to left. Thus he could create a paradox in the garden: for the walls that enclosed and limited his space also served to extend it magically beyond all bounds.

As a painter and connoisseur, Ji Cheng would also, however unconsciously, in gardens as in art, have looked for a quality described as *qi yun sheng dong*. This, the "first principle" of painting, was formulated by Xie He, a fifth-century art theorist, and has been interpretatively developed by others ever since. Translated by Alexander Soper as "animation through spirit consonance," it means two things: first, that the *qi* or "vital spirit" of every part of a painting must "vibrate" with the *qi* of every other part; second, that the *qi* of the painted forms must respond to that of the real forms as they exist outside the painting. It thus implies both inner consistency, by which themes set up harmonious vibrations among themselves, and a mystical realism, whereby the artist magically captures the animating spirit of nature itself. For garden designers this is immensely important. The garden microcosm is not to be merely a reproduction of nature in miniature, but a poetic, lyrical and artistic interpretation of it, with its own "vital spirit." This is why Ji Cheng is adamant that, in garden design, there are "principles but no fixed formulae." The designer must seek the essence lying behind the forms—the "mountainness" of all mountains rather than the shape of a specific range. Above all he must feel the specific qualities of his own site and follow where it leads him. Thus Ji Cheng teaches general principles by suggestion rather than by rule, encouraging the reader, through evocative descriptions, to release his own creative imagination.

Naturally, success in this is not for everyone: "the exceptional takes effort and deep understanding," and even then (most practically), "after the inspiration of genius, completion depends on the labor of man." Nevertheless, Ji Cheng is encouraging, for he believes that when "you have the real thing within you... it will become real," and that his reader will "know when it is right when it moves [him]." And this, perhaps, is the key; for within its own small space a garden must make possible a whole range of emotions that otherwise could be felt only in nature. Thus the garden designer strives to heighten his effects by contrast and juxtaposition—high leading to low, open to closed, narrow to wide, light to dark—in a constant, delicate pairing, on an infinity of levels, that echoes the elemental force of the *yin* and *yang*. In practice the designer manages so to confuse the visitor about how he came in, where he is and how he is to get out, and at the same time so to delight and lull his senses, that the space of his little garden seems to extend indefinitely.

The Literary Dimension

It extends indefinitely also in a literary sense. For an educated Chinese, part of the pleasure of a garden lies in the savoring of *vers d'occasion* written by previous visitors and engraved on stone tablets let into the walls. Just as a great landscape painting acquires, over time, the calligraphy of connoisseurs as colophons around its margins, so the garden acquires history, life and meaning from poems that record the feelings of those who, maybe a hundred years before, enjoyed the same sights and sounds and scents as are still there.

In addition, paired couplets were written in expressive calligraphy on each side of gateways, and the names of pavilions or courtyards, on wooden tablets above their entrances. Choosing such names often provided a delightful game in which scholars could cap each other with a brilliant literary allusion or an apt metaphor. They set the mood for each new part of the garden, probing layers of literary recollection, adding new insights to old meanings. And the supple and powerful strokes of the calligraphy in which they were written echoed the shapes of leaves and branches all around: man and nature harmonized in art.

For the foreigner, however, the "magical realism" of China's few remaining old gardens may still be elusive. They were, after all, meant to be savored over a lifetime, and they often took a lifetime to make. For a woman with bound feet, the garden of her family house (if she was lucky enough to have one) might represent the sum total of her freedom. In traditional China a group of friends might have spent a whole afternoon in the corner of one courtyard watching the sun move round on a rock—revealing in the cracks and fissures lions perhaps, or cranes, or even the faces of Immortals—or another, in autumn, "appreciating the chrysanthemums" or, in the late spring, the peonies.

Small wonder, then, if tourists find themselves confused: a quick run through the watery labyrinth of, for instance, the Zhuo Zheng Yuan can lead only to visual indigestion, while in the last six or seven years the garden have been so swamped with visitors one is lucky to see them at all. Chinese and foreigners, old and young, they swarm over the Immortal's rocks, photograph each other on the bridges and litter the lakes with a film of orange peel and cigarette ends. Public lavatories and cafés occupy some of the pavilions, and the earth is stamped dry and lifeless by a thousand feet.

Perhaps sometime the authorities will build more public parks with playgrounds and cafés in the old cities of Jiangnan, and these will provide more space for many of those who now use the gardens without much noticing where they are. Then perhaps, the authorities who have gardens in their care will limit the numbers and even, as they do in Japan, require one to book in advance the pleasures of a garden stroll. With so many people it is hard to know how best to preserve the balance between man and nature, already irreparably altered on our planet. And perhaps the shattered tranquility of these gardens is no more than a just reflection of this. At any rate for the moment, the world of men has breached the lime-washed walls. Ji Cheng, I think, would have bowed his head in sadness.

10 (following page) Rock with bamboo, pine and orchids *(cymbidium)*, Liu He Ta (Pagoda of the Six Harmonies), Hangzhou.

The
CRAFT *of* GARDENS

Ji Cheng

FOREWORD *by Zheng Yuanxun*

The various arts of ancient times have all been handed down in writing, so why has the art of designing gardens alone not had a written tradition? It has been said: "Different things are suitable for different gardens; there is no single hard and fast rule, so there is no way that it can be handed down in writing."

What is meant by saying that different things are suitable for different gardens? Because of the royal birth of the Jianwen Emperor of Liang, the Flowery Forest came into being;[1] because of Jilun's wealth, he was able to create the Golden Valley;[2] but because Chen Zhongzi was so poor, he could only afford a small vegetable garden at Yuling.[3] Different things were appropriate for these people according to their different circumstances of nobility or humble birth, wealth or poverty: it would be inconceivable to have things the other way around.

If a site has no remote and lofty hills or flourishing woods like those of the Orchid Pavilion, yet you insist on applying the name of the Serpentine to it;[4] or if there is absolutely no sign of such sights as the Deer Enclosure or Dappled Apricots, but you baselessly boast it as another Wangchuan,[5] this is even worse than the Bogeywoman smearing on powder and rouge, and succeeding only in making herself uglier still.[6]

Different types of ground, too, require different treatment, and this should be given careful consideration. The owner must be sure of having the hills and valleys already there in his heart, and then the completed work may be either elaborate or simple, as he wishes. Otherwise, if he forces out something artificial, and leaves it all up to the builders and tilers, the streams will not give the appearance of an undulating ribbon, the hills will not overlap and wind in and out of one another, and the trees and plants will not give each other shade in a suitable way. How, then, can the attraction of the garden grow upon the viewer day by day?

The most unfortunate thing is if the landowner has the hills and valleys in his heart but cannot express his concept to the workmen, while the workmen can follow instructions but are not creative, and just have to stick to their plumb-lines and ink-marks. If they thus force the owner to abandon his original concept of hills and valleys to follow their ideas, is that not a great pity? But Ji Wufou has changed all that: he goes by the concept, not by a fixed set of rules, something which most people cannot achieve. And he is even better at directing operations successfully, so that the stubborn becomes flexible and the blocked flows freely: this is really something to be glad about.

I am one of Wufou's oldest friends, and I know that he often feels frustrated that a remnant of water and a broken-off piece of mountain give

11 (facing page) Wen Zhengming, *Gathering at the Orchid Pavilion* (Palace Museum, Beijing).

no scope for his accumulated skills; he would dearly love to set out all the ten great mountains of China in one area, and direct a squad of all the mighty laborers of the empire; and to collect together all sorts of exotic, jewel-like flowers and plants, ancient trees and sacred birds to be arranged by him, giving the whole earth a totally new appearance. What a joy this would be to him! But alas, there is no landowner with sufficiently grand ideas!

Does this mean then that Wufou can operate only on a grand scale and not on a small one? No, this is not the case, Different things are suitable both for different gardens and for different people, and no one is Wufou's equal in making appropriate use of what is available. When I was building a mansion to the south of the city-wall of Jiangdu, among reedy marshes and banks of willows, the site was only a few yards wide in either direction, but Wufou had only to make some simple arrangements, and it became a magical secluded retreat. I can claim to know a little about garden design and construction myself, but beside Wufou, I feel as clumsy as a cuckoo that cannot even build its own nest.[7]

There are many distinguished connoisseurs in the world who wish to build country retreats and gardens in which they can enjoy roaming freely in a small space; all these people cannot fail to ask Wufou's advice. Unfortunately he cannot divide himself up and distribute himself in all directions to respond to them, but perhaps his compiling of *The Craft of Gardens* can compensate for this. Still, I shall always feel sad that Wufou's knowledge and skill cannot really be handed on; what can be handed on is only a set of rules, which is as much as to say that nothing has been handed on. But if his rules can be applied flexibly, without departing from his principles, then this sort of transmission, which at least gives people something to go by, will still be better than nothing at all.

Today's genius of national status will become a standard for later generations to emulate. Who can say that his book will not become an object of praise in the mouths of all, rivalling even the "Record of All Crafts" in the *Rites of Zhou*?[8]

Written on the first day of the fifth month,
in the Yihai year of the Chongzhen era [1635]
by his friend Zheng Yuanxun in the Garden of Shade.[9]

12 (facing page) "A remnant of water and a broken-off piece of mountain... a magical, secluded retreat." Lotus pond at Qiu Xia Pu (Nursery Garden of Autumn Vapors), Jiading, near Shanghai. The first garden on this site was built in the sixteenth century for a family surnamed Gong. It subsequently became the garden of the township temple, and in the eighteenth century was combined with the "East Garden" next door, which belonged to the Shen family, to make the present Qiu Xia Pu. The pillar in the middle of the pond is of Buddhist significance.

ON THE "CRAFT" *by Ruan Dacheng*

As a young man it was my dream to live the hermit's life like Xiang Changping and Qin Qing,[10] but to my chagrin I was constrained by my official career. Fortunately I was dismissed from office, and so thought that I should be able to carry out my original intention. But at this time there were disturbances all over the country, and moreover I could not abandon the care of my parents to take off on any free and easy wanderings.[11] Was I then to be restricted to our chicken-runs and pig-sties, and to our family gatherings?

The Luan River was near where we lived, so one day I took a boat to a place between the Wu Garden and Willow Pool, and stayed there overnight.[12] I had a most pleasant, quiet time there. What I liked was the way that this place took fine hills and valleys and managed to enclose them within the small confines of a fence. I could after all combine my love of natural scenery with the attention due to my parents without moving from one place, and would be able to laugh at those people who travelled far and wide through clouds and mist!

This place had a garden, and there was a book about gardens called the *Craft*, and the person whose *Craft* this was, was Ji Wufou of Songling;[13] moreover, the person who had given this book the name of *Craft* was none other than my friend Cao Yuanfu of Gushu.[14]

Wufou is a most straightforward man, of remarkable character and talents; stilted and formal behavior stands no chance in his presence. His poems and paintings are just like his personality; no wonder Yuanfu is so fond of them.

So I decided to clear the weeds from a piece of marginal land and have it set out with hills and water, to make a place where I could enjoy reading and playing the lute. On festive days, I would accompany my parents, leaning on their walking-sticks or riding in litters, and arrange for them to watch dancing there. I myself would wear a coat of many colors,[15] sing a hermit's song of magic herbs, and offer my parents a brimming goblet of wine to wish them long life; thus, pleasantly, I intended to spend the rest of my days.

Remarkable indeed is Master Ji's ability to give pleasure in just the way I wished; I must fill another glass and raise it to him. As the singing dies away and the moon comes out, and the peaks in the garden are shrouded in quietness, I call Yuanfu to witness: how can he fail to repond?

> I took up my pen to write this in the fourth month
> of the Jiaxu year in the Chongzhen era [1634],
> when the garden was filled with blossom
> and the birds were like friends to me.
> Ruan Dacheng of Stone Nest.[16]

14 A view similar to that which Ruan Dacheng must have seen as he approached the Wu Garden: the outside of the Qiu Xia Pu.

13 (facing page) Wen Zhengming, *The Studio of True Appreciation*, 1557 (Shanghai Museum).

Author's Preface

As a young man I was known as a painter. I was by nature interested in seeking out the unusual; since I derived most pleasure from the brushes of Guan Tong and Jing Hao, I paid homage to their style in all my work.[17]

I travelled between the region of Peking in the north and the old land of Chu in the south,[18] and in middle-age returned to my home region of Wu,[19] where I decided to settle at Zhenjiang. Zhenjiang is surrounded by the most beautiful scenery, and people in the area who cared about such things collected rocks, and arranged those with interesting shapes among bamboos and trees to make artificial mountains. One day I happened on some of these, and burst out laughing at them. When somebody asked me what I was laughing at, I answered, "It has been said that art imitates life, but why do you not imitate the appearance of real mountains, instead of those heaps of fist-shaped stones which country people put up to welcome the God of Spring?"[20] "Could you do any better yourself?" they asked, so I arranged some rocks into the shape of a cliff; everyone who saw it exclaimed, "What a magnificent mountain!" and word of it spread far and near.

It so happened that Lord Wu Youyu, the Civil and Finance Officer of Changzhou, heard the story and invited me to call on him.[21] His lordship had some property to the east of the city-wall which was barely fifteen *mu*[22] in area and had once been a garden belonging to the Khan of Wen under the Yuan dynasty.[23] His lordship instructed me thus: "These ten *mu* will be set aside for a residence, and for the remaining five I should like to follow descriptions of the ancient 'Garden of Solitary Delight' created by Sima Guang, the Duke of Wen."[24]

I could see that the contours of the property rose very high; as one tracked the stream to its source, it led deep into the hillside. Tall trees reached to touch the heavens, while twisting branches brushed the earth. "To make a garden here, " I said, "one should not only pile up rocks to emphasize the height, but excavate the earth to increase the depth, in proportion with these tall trees scattered on the hillside here, with their roots curled around sheer rocks just as in a painting. Following the course of the stream we should construct pavilions and terraces, whose reflections will be scattered on the surface of the pond, with winding gullies and flying galleries leading on from them, so that people will be taken beyond anything they could have imagined."

16 Anonymous 10th-century artist, *Meeting to Play Chess in the Mountains* (Liaoning Provincial Museum). This painting, recovered from a tomb dated to c. 980, reflects the artistic style of the time when painters such as Guan Tong and Jing Hao, so admired by Ji Cheng, were active.

15 (facing page) Ji Cheng's hometown: a general view over the modern city of Zhenjiang.

17 "Pile up rocks to emphasize the height, excavate the earth to increase the depth." Ji Chang Yuan, Wuxi, Jiangsu province.

18 "Pavilions and terraces, whose reflections will be scattered on the surface of the pond." Ji Chang Yuan, Wuxi.

19 "Flying galleries," Ge Yuan.

20 An "artificial mountain" such as Ji Cheng might have constructed. Note also the decorative paving. Qiu Xia Pu, Jiading.

When the work was completed his lordship was delighted and said, "From entering to leaving, one actually only walks a mile and a half, but you would think that we had collected together in this small space all the famous sights South of the River."[25] Among all this there were also some small buildings—really just tiny cottages on a fragment of mountain—in which I felt I had managed to express all the unusual ideas in my imagination, so that I felt particularly satisfied with my achievement.

At that time Secretary Wang Shiheng[26] also commissioned me to design a garden to the west of Luan River,[27] and as it seems that the result was in accordance with his intentions, both this garden and the one that I designed for Lord Wu Youyu became equally famous north and south of the Yangtze River.

In my leisure hours I collected my sketches and notes under the title "The Care of Gardens." On his travels Master Cao Yuanfu of Gushu came to visit Secretary Wang's garden,[28] and the owner and I accompanied him on a stroll through the garden, where he was invited to stay for a couple of days. Master Cao praised it over and over again, saying it was just like a painting by Jing Hao or Guan Tong, and asking if I could put my techniques down in writing.[29] So I brought my notes out to show him, and he said, "This has not been heard or seen for a thousand ages! Why call it merely 'The Care of Gardens'? This is your personal creation, sir; you should call it 'The Craft of Gardens.'"

Recorded in the Xinwei year of the Chongzhen era [1631]
at the end of autumn,
by the Negative Daoist Ji Cheng
at his leisure in the Huye Hall.

The THEORY
of CONSTRUCTION

Generally, in construction, responsibility is given to a "master" who assembles a team of craftsmen; for is there not a proverb that though three-tenths of the work is the workmen's, seven-tenths is the master's? By "master" here I do not mean the owner of the property, but the man who is master of his craft. The skill of Lu Ban or the fine artistry of Lu Yun in ancient times should not lead us to think that they actually wielded the axe or adze themselves.[30] If an ordinary workman merely carves skillfully or sets up the framework of a building competently, with pillars and crossbeams, so that it is firm and immovable, it is quite correct to call him by the expression "a mere mechanic."[31]

So whenever a building is undertaken, the ground must first be studied and the foundations established, then the span and depth of the rooms decided upon; widths must be calculated, curves introduced in appropriate places and angles squared elsewhere; and all this is the responsibility of the master. His craftsmanship is shown in the design of something appropriate and fitting to the site, so he cannot stick too closely to convention. If the ground for the foundations slopes or falls steeply away, why should every part of the building necessarily be parallel or at right angles to every other part? And why should the structure of the house be confined to three or five room spans of a certain depth from front to back?[32] To add an extra half span to form an alcove may look natural and elegant. This is exactly the sort of thing implied by the phrase "seven-tenths of the work is the master's."

In fact, the master in charge of constructing a garden residence should really account for nine-tenths of the work, and the workmen he employs for only one-tenth. Why is this? Skill in landscape design is shown in the ability to "follow" and "borrow from" the existing scenery and lie of the land, and artistry is shown in the feeling of suitability created. This is even further beyond the powers of mere workmen, as well as beyond the control of the landowner. The owner must obtain the services of the right person, and not throw his money away.

Following the existing lie of the land may mean any of these skills: designing in accordance with the rise and fall of the natural contours, to accentuate their intrinsic form; or lopping branches from trees that block the view and using rocks to direct the flow of a spring, so that each borrows value from the other. Where a pavilion would be appropriate, build a pavilion, and where a gazebo, build a gazebo.[33] It does not matter if the paths are hidden away; in fact they should be laid out so that they twist and turn with the land; this is what is meant by artistry through suitability.

21 (facing page) Builders at work, Hangzhou, 1986.

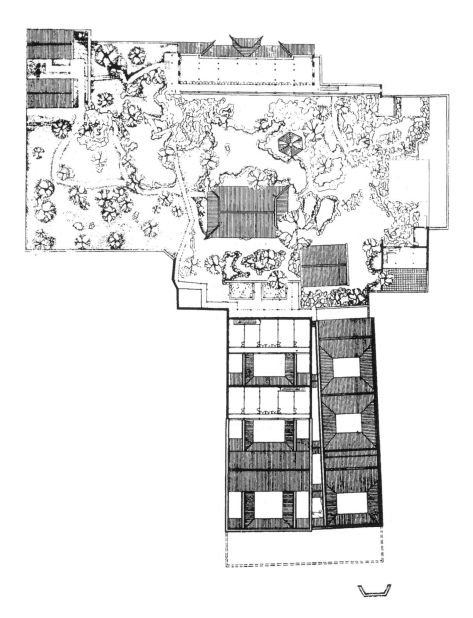

22 Ground plan of Ge Yuan, Yangzhou, from Chen Congzhou, *Yangzhou Yuanlin* (*Gardens of Yangzhou*). Note what a prominent part buildings play even within the area of the garden itself; the actual dwelling-houses are in the area extending to the south.

23 View from upper walkway of northernmost building, Ge Yuan, "borrowing" the scenery of trees and buildings beyond the garden's own boundaries.

To borrow from the scenery means that although the interior of a garden is distinct from what lies outside it, as long as there is a good view you need not be concerned whether this is close by or far away, whether clear mountains raise their beauty in the distance or a purple-walled temple rises into the sky nearby. Wherever the view within your sight is vulgar, block it off, but where it is beautiful, take advantage of it; never mind if it is just of empty fields, make use of it all as a misty background. This is what is known as skill in fitting in with the form of the land. However, even if the form is fitting and the design follows the lie of the land, but the owner still does not get the right person to carry out the work, and in addition is reluctant to spend money when necessary, then any work which may have been done previously will be wasted along with his present efforts. Even if a latter-day Lu Ban or Lu Yun were to exist, they could never become known to future ages.[34] I too was afraid that my achievements would be swept away on the tide of history, so I have illustrated my designs in the following text, to be shared by fellow-enthusiasts.

24 Another type of borrowed view: the outside is partially glimpsed through the "openwork" wall, Zhenjiang.

On Gardens

Generally, in the construction of gardens, whether in the countryside or on the outskirts of a city, a secluded location is the best. In clearing woodland one should select and prune the tangled undergrowth; where a fine piece of natural scenery occurs one should make the most of it. Where there is a mountain torrent one may cultivate orchids and angelica together.[35] Paths should be lined with the "three auspicious things" whose property it is to symbolize eternity.[36] The surrounding wall should be concealed under creepers, and rooftops should emerge here and there above the tops of the trees. If you climb a tower on a hill-top to gaze into the distance, nothing but beauty will meet your eye; if you seek a secluded spot among banks of bamboo, intoxication will flood your heart. The pillars of your verandah should be tall and widely spaced; your windows and doors should give an unimpeded view.

The view should include a watery expanse of many acres and contain the changing brilliance of the four seasons.[37] The shadow of phoenix trees should cover the ground, the shade of pagoda trees pattern the walls.[38] Willows should be set along the embankments, plum trees around the buildings; reeds should be planted among the bamboos. A long channel should be dug out for the stream. With hillsides as tapestries and mountains as screens, set up a thousand feet of emerald slopes; though man-made, they will look like something naturally created. Shadowy temples should appear through round windows, like a painting by the Younger Li.[39] Lofty summits should be heaped up from rocks cut to look as if they were painted with slash strokes,[40] uneven like the half-cliffs of Dachi.[41] If you can have a Buddhist monastery as your neighbor, the chanting of Sanskrit will come to your ears; if distant mountain ranges can be included in the view, their fresh beauty is there for you to absorb. With the grey-violet of vaporous morning or pale evening mist, the cry of cranes will drift to your pillow.[42] Among the white duckweed and red polygonum,[43] flocks of gulls will gather beside your jetty. To see the mountains, ride on a bamboo litter; to visit the river, lean on an oaken staff. Slantwise soar the parapets, crosswise strides the long rainbow bridge. You need not envy Wang Wei's Wangchuan; Jilun's Golden Valley will count for nothing.[44] Is Xiaoxia the only bay worthy of the name?[45] There are more open spaces here than Cangchun.

If you raise deer they can roam freely about; if you breed fish they can

26 Huang Gongwang (1269-1354), *Clearing after Snow on the Nine Peaks*, 1349 (Palace Museum, Beijing).

25 (facing page) "A secluded spot among...bamboos." Ge Yuan, Yangzhou.

27 "Rooftops should emerge here and there above the tops of the trees." Hu Pao Si, Hangzhou.

be caught. In cool summer pavilions you can play drinking-games, mix ice with your drinks, and feel the breeze rising among the bamboos and trees. In warm winter apartments you can gather round the stove, and melt snow to make your tea while the water bubbles in the wine-warmer. Your troubles will be quenched along with your thirst. The night-rain patters on the plantain leaves like a mermaid's tears.[46] The dawn breeze soughs through the willows, as if caressing Xiaoman's slender waist.[47] Transplant some bamboos in front of your window, and set aside some pear trees to form a courtyard. The scene is bathed in moonlight, the wind whispers. The moonlight plays quietly over lute and books, the wind ruffles a half-circle of autumn water. We feel a pure atmosphere around our table and seats; the common dust of the world is far from our souls.[48]

Do not feel restricted to the conventional sizes of windows, but use them as you feel appropriate.[49] Visualize the balustrades as if they were in a painting, following the lines of their surroundings. The designs you create should be fresh in style; you should reject the old conventions of monumental building. Yours may not be so "magnificent," but it will be just right for something small and private.

I SITUATION

In laying the foundations of a garden you should not feel any restriction as to the direction it faces; the shape of the ground will have its natural highs and lows. There should be something to arouse interest as you pass through the

28 "Cool summer pavilions." Zhan Yuan, Nanjing.

gate; you should follow the natural lie of the land to obtain interesting views, whether the garden lies beside wooded hills or abuts on a stream or pool. To make good use of unusual features adjacent to the city you must keep far from major thoroughfares. To find outstanding sites in the local villages, you should avail yourself of the uneven height of deep woods. If you place your garden in a country village you can gaze into the distance; if it is in a market town it will be more convenient to reach from your home. If you are constructing the garden from scratch, then it will be easy to lay out the foundations, but for immediate effect you can do no more than plant some willows and transplant bamboo. There is more skill involved in redesigning an old garden, although you have the natural advantages of ancient trees and profusely growing flowers.

Some gardens are naturally rectangular, some rounded, others linear, others curving. If the garden is lengthy and curving it should take the form of a circular jade.[50] If it is straight and wide it should suggest spreading clouds. If it is high and square you should make use of pavilions and terraces. If it is low and concave you can dig out pools and ponds. When you are taking geomantic readings to locate the garden,[51] it is advantageous to have an area of water, and when starting to work on the main plan, you should go straight to the water source. You should dredge the course of the stream and find out where the water comes from or flows to.

If you can place a building beside the stream, it can cross from bank to bank and support an open pavilion. If the building has a lane lying close beside it, you can use the space above the lane to make an overhanging walkway.[52]

If the garden is to be adorned with scenery belonging to another landowner, providing there is a single thread of connection between them, then it is not really separate, and it is quite appropriate to "borrow" the view. If it faces on to a neighbor's flowers, however small a glimpse of them is to be had, they can be called into play and one can enjoy an unlimited springtime. If you build a bridge across water which would otherwise form a barrier you can then construct a separate cottage worthy of a painting. If you pile up rocks to make a surrounding wall, you can have something comparable to a mountain retreat.

If there are trees which have stood for many years that would get in the way of the eaves or walls of your building, you should set the

29 (above left) An "Overhanging walkway" similar to the kind mentioned by Ji Cheng can be seen on the building in the background, He Yuan. The building on the right could be used for the performance of plays to entertain the owner and his family or guests.

30 (above right) Upper walkway, He Yuan.

foundations back a bit, or else lop off a few branches to avoid the roof, for it is comparatively easy to construct carved beams and soaring pillars, but it takes a long time to grow pagoda trees old enough to give real shade and bamboo groves like a mass of green jade.

To sum up, if one chooses an appropriate site, the construction of the garden will follow naturally.

1 Sites among Mountain Forests

The most picturesque position for a garden is among tree-clad hills, where there are high slopes and hollows, winding fissures and deep gullies, tall overhanging cliffs and flat level ground, and the site has developed its own natural attractions without the jarring note of human handiwork.

You can go into a deep, mysterious gully, dredge out a spring and dig out a watercourse at the bottom; then excavate the hollows and the foot of the hill, banking up earth on which to build rooms and walkways.

All kinds of trees will reach up to the sky, and the tops of towers will appear and disappear among the clouds. Flowers in profusion will cover the ground, and terraces will rise at varying heights above the surface of the water.

If there are unfordable torrents, build bridges over them, and where there are soaring cliffs, construct stairways up them. Approach the scenery at your ease, and in seclusion explore the springtime. The birds are seeking their companions, the deer are joining with their mates. Along the fence waft gusts of the spring breeze, bringing the scent of flowers; around the gate winds a band of rippling water. The path through the bamboos leads into the unknown. The pinewood retreat is hidden away. Here the splashing of the ripples merges far away with the wing-beat of the dancing cranes.[53] You can brush away the clouds from before your steps, and on the peak one can almost touch the moon.

A thousand peaks are ringed with turquoise; a myriad valleys run with azure. If you are willing to ride in Tao Qian's litter, what need is there for Xie Lingyun's climbing-boots?[54]

2 Urban Sites

Inner-city sites are not intrinsically suitable for gardens; if you construct a garden there, it must be in a place as secluded and out of the way as possible, so that although it may be close to vulgar surroundings the gate can be shut to keep out the hubbub.

Long, winding paths should lead the way into the garden, and the battlements of the city-wall should be just visible in the distance above bamboos and trees. A winding moat should be dug around the edge of the garden, with rainbow bridges stretching over it from rustic gates.

Extensive courtyards can be planted with phoenix trees; curving embankments are suitable for willow-trees. It may be difficult to build villas in other places, but here it is as easy as growing the trees. The buildings

31 "Extensive courtyards can be planted…" He Yuan.

33 "Through an open window one can see the delicate shadows of plantain leaves." Ou Yuan, Suzhou.

should follow the lie of the land; watercourses should be dredged out and made firm with banks of stone. Pavilions should be sited where they have a good view, and flowers planted near them to smile in the spring breeze.

Open-sided pavilions may be shaded by paulownia trees, where clear pools envelop the moon. Washed clear of mist and rain, the moonlight falls on the book-lined study walls.

A pure white waterfall cascades like floating gauze into the mirror of a pool. Green hills stand like an encircling screen beyond the city.

Peonies may be grown against a trellis, but roses should not have a support.[55] You may train them over rocks but avoid weaving them into a hedge, for if they are tied back for a long time and over-pruned, they can never survive without damage.

Even a small hill may be very effective, and a handful of rocks can stir the emotions.

Through an open window one can see the delicate shadows of plantain leaves, and on the twisting cliffs the thick gnarled roots of pines.

This proves that the hermit's life in a city far surpasses a distant mountain retreat.[56] If you can find seclusion in a noisy place, there is no need to yearn for places far from where you live. Whenever you have some leisure you are already at your goal, and whenever the mood takes you, you can set off with your friends for a walk.

3 Village Sites

Among the ancients, those who enjoyed the pastoral life used to live among open farmland.[57] Nowadays those who pillow their heads on the hillsides choose the most attractive of rural villages, surrounded by wattle fences, with mulberry and jute growing everywhere around them. They dredge streams to make waterways and shore up dikes to plant willows. From their gateways they can inspect the crops, and from their verandahs step straight into their vegetable gardens.

34 Vegetation on a "twisting cliff." Ge Yuan.

For every ten parts of land, three should be made into a pond, of irregular shape so that it is interesting, and preferably made by dredging out an existing stream. Of the remaining seven-tenths, four should be built up with earth—how high or low is of no importance—and be planted with bamboo in a harmonious way.

If the buildings are set in an open and uncluttered plan, green fields will still be seen to spread around them, while the shade of flowering plants will seem like an extra barrier to the outside. When you pile up rocks it need not be obvious that the mountain is artificial, and when you come to a bridge it should seem like a natural ford across the water. Paths will develop naturally among the peach and plum trees, and the buildings and terraces will grow to look like a painting.

The surrounding fence should be woven of thorn bushes, with a little gap left in it for the dogs to go out and greet visitors. A winding path should go round by the fence, with the moss trodden down where the garden-boy has swept the leaves.

As autumn draws to a close the honey has still not been taken from the hive; when the harvest is finished the first thing to check is the food store for the cranes.

In your peaceful life of leisure you need not worry about getting enough rice or millet to eat, but you will not refuse a walk through wind and snow to buy wine. Returning to the woods in fulfillment of his heart's desire, the old gardener will be more than satisfied.[58]

37 "A handful of rocks can stir the emotions." He Yuan.

35 (facing page top) Entrance to Zhan Yuan, Nanjing.

36 (facing page bottom) Borrowed view over the West Lake to a distant bridge. Fenyang Villa, Hangzhou.

4 Sites in Uninhabited Countryside

In choosing sites on the further outskirts of a town, you should keep to level ridges and winding valleys, rolling banks and lofty forests, where deep water-courses reach back to their source, and bridges stride at right angles across the water. It is no distance from the city and you can come and go whenever you feel like it; this is happiness indeed. Within the garden you must bear in mind the ups and downs of the greater landscape, and grasp the scale of the area. For the surrounding wall, remember the method of tamping earth between boards; and in building an embankment, copy the Xi Jia Pond.[59] When you begin to clear a virgin site you should bring in a long stream, and in opening out a vista you should keep all the different shrubs you can. If you dig a channel along the bottom of a wall but fear that the water may undermine the wall, you can arrange boulders to support it; if you train creepers across a ford, you can cross by means of this aerial bridge. Where the wind breeds sharp cold, you can plant peach trees in the shelter of the willows along the curving banks of the stream. Where the moonlight is dim and faint, plant bamboos beyond the plum trees around your lodging. In this way you can increase the mystery of the place and engulf yourself in an even deeper emotion. Two or three rooms do what they can to hold the warmth of spring, while one or two places provide a shelter from the summer's heat. On the other side of the woods the turtledoves call for rain;[60] on the far bank of the river, horses whinny into the wind. As the flowers fall, summon the garden-boy to sweep them up, and entertain your guests deep among the bamboos. Anyone may enjoy the garden as they please, without the owner questioning them; as the visitors fulfill their wish, they need not announce their names. You should appreciate the clear tones of breeze and moon. Don't commit crimes against the hills and forests. A man of sensibility will never treat them irreverently, but any vulgar comments must be swept away.[61]

5 Sites beside a Mansion House

If there is the merest fraction of land beside or behind your mansion, you can construct a garden there; not only is it convenient for enjoying your leisure moments in, but it can also be regarded as an excellent cordon for protecting the house. Excavate a pool and dig out a moat, arrange rocks and build up a mountain, construct a gate to welcome arriving visitors, and keep a path open to connect it to the nearest building. With bamboo growing elegantly and trees flourishing, with shady willows and bright flowers, an area of five *mu* is not a restriction; in fact you can rival Lord Wen's Garden of Solitary Delight.[62] Throughout the four seasons never let the flowers fade, and you will be able to wander through them together with your pageboy Little Jade.[63]

During the days of blossoming mornings and nights of moonlit dusks, when your household is serving you with wine, you may reveal the treasures concealed in your seraglio;[64] when guests gather together for a poetry contest,

you can make them drink a forfeit of three ladles of wine as in "The Golden Valley."[65] With people chanting stanzas all around you, it will be like a little paradise. You will constantly have your couch strewn with lutes and books, and never be without the wraith-like stems of bamboo.

If you build your hut by a mountain torrent, it seems you are sure to find peace and quiet. But if you bring the mountains to your home, what need is there to search for remote places? Your mansion will inherit the lofty style of the poet Xie Tiao,[66] and the hilltops will be pierced with the echoing whistle of the hermit Sun Deng.[67]

When looking for plum blossoms you can do without Meng Haoran's donkey,[68] and when you boil water from snow you will be accompanied by a concubine as lovely as Tao Yi's.[69] You can entrust your purified body to the Dark and the Yellow,[70] and then you need not consider your attitude towards other people.[71]

You would never think that a garden which will last a thousand years could be made by the hand of man, who lasts but a hundred. The pleasure and relaxation of it are enough in themselves, but more, the garden will protect your mansion and keep it free from any disturbance.

38 "In opening out a vista, you should keep all the different shrubs you can." Yi Yuan (Elegant Garden), Nanxiang, near Shanghai. This garden was originally constructed in the Ming dynasty for a family surnamed Min, by a garden designer called Zhu Sansong (Three Pines Zhu).

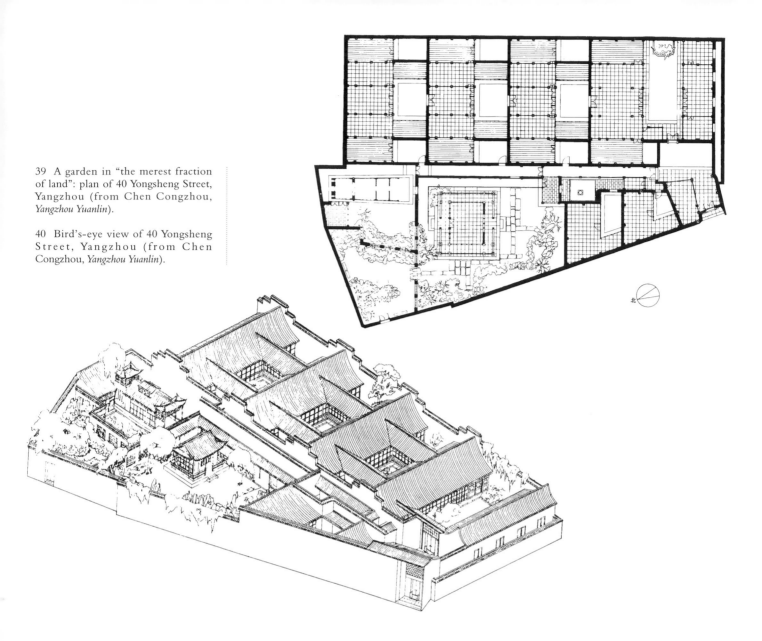

39 A garden in "the merest fraction of land": plan of 40 Yongsheng Street, Yangzhou (from Chen Congzhou, *Yangzhou Yuanlin*).

40 Bird's-eye view of 40 Yongsheng Street, Yangzhou (from Chen Congzhou, *Yangzhou Yuanlin*).

41 Wen Zhengming, *Tea Tasting at Mount Hui*, 1518 (Palace Museum, Beijing). Like Tao Yi and his concubine, Ji Cheng's contemporaries valued the connoisseurship of tea. Mount Hui, near the town of Wuxi, was famous for its pure spring water.

6 River and Lakeside Sites

On the banks of rivers and the shores of lakes, beyond the dense willows and sparse reeds, a few small, neat cottages can make a fine sight. The misty water spreads into the distance, cloudy mountains shimmer on the horizon, fishing boats bob up and down, water birds soar through the air.

The roof-tops are hidden in the drifting layers of mist; terraces rise to meet the new moon. As you strike a rhythm on your lute the clouds flow in unison; as you pass the cup around, the sunset mist lingers for a while. How like it is to the Peak of Gou:[72] you could almost accompany Zijin on his flute! If you wish to make a copy of the Jasper Lake, you can expect King Mu to entertain you to a feast.[73]

To find such relaxation—this is happiness; to know how to enjoy life is to become an Immortal.[74]

II LAYOUT

The most important element in the layout of gardens is the siting of the principal buildings. The primary consideration is the view, and it is all the better if the buildings can also face south.[75] If there are some tall trees

42 Layout: part of the He Yuan, showing the combination of water, rocks, plants, and buildings. The main building (to the right of the picture) does in fact face due south, over the pool.

43 "A curving bay of willows…cleanses the soul." Qiu Xia Pu, Jiading.

around, then keep one or two of them growing in the courtyards. When you build walls you must spread them widely and preserve plenty of open space within them, so that you can arrange and lay out the place exactly as you wish. Once you have picked a site for the main buildings, you can use the remaining space for the construction of pavilions and terraces. Their form should follow what is appropriate, and you should cultivate the plants around them very carefully.

In choosing the direction the buildings face in, do not be bound by what the geomancer tells you. But in positioning a gateway, it must be square on to the main hall in its courtyard. Build up mountains from the excavated soil, and form embankments along the edges of the ponds. A curving bay of willows in the moonlight cleanses the soul in its clear waves; a ten-mile expanse of lotuses in the breeze wafts its fragrance to your hidden study. Weave a wattle fence and grow chrysanthemums, like Warden Tao in days of yore;[76] hoe the hillside and plant plum trees, following in the ancient footsteps of Lord Yu.[77] Find a secluded place to which to transplant bamboo; plant flowers to highlight the scenery. Though peach and plum cannot speak, they seem to bring news of the path to wisdom,[78] and the reflections upside

down in the pond make you think you are entering a mermaid's palace. A single stream seems to hold the promise of autumn coolness; ranks of shady trees cut off the summer heat. You should let the water flow freely as if it had no end, and where it blocks your path, build a bridge across it.

In clearing woodland you should take thought and do it in a rational way, putting up small buildings at intervals. Walkways should be winding and towers lofty, giving rise to the feeling expressed in Wang Wei's line, "The river flows beyond the edge of the world," and in harmony with his words, "The prospect of the mountains lies between being and non-being."[79] As the mood takes you, you can gaze into the distance over the flourishing plain, or look far away to lofty peaks for a more impressive sight. High mounds can be further heightened and low-lying places should be dug deeper still.

1 The Great Hall [*ting tang*]

In ancient times the standard layout for the great hall was either five or three spans.[80] You should consider the amount of space available; it may also be possible to have four spans or even four and a half. If it is not possible

44 "Lotuses in the breeze waft their fragrance to your hidden study." Qiu Xia Pu, Jiading.

to extend it so far, then three and a half is also acceptable. Whether the building is secretive and convoluted, or open and accessible front and back, all depends on this half span, which gives the impression of a region of illusion.[81] The creation of any garden must always be undertaken according to this formula.

2 Towers [*lou ge*]

The siting of a tower, according to convention, should be behind the great hall. Why not build it in the midst of hills and waters so that it can be described as being both two storeys and three storeys? From below, looking up, it is a high tower; from halfway up the hill it will resemble a one-storey house, but if you "ascend another storey" you will really be able to "see for a thousand miles."[82]

3 Gate Towers [*men lou*]

Although buildings in gardens generally have no fixed orientation in common, the foundations of gate towers alone should always be aligned with the orientation of the great hall and built in a suitable relation to it.

46 A main building of the type Ji Cheng refers to as a Great Hall: the Si Mian Ting or Four-sided Hall, He Yuan. This is a building of three spans.

45 (facing page) "A single stream seems to hold the promise of autumn coolness; ranks of shady trees cut off the summer heat." Yi Yuan, Nanxiang. The building in the background fits Ji Cheng's description of an ideal study (p. 60).

47 A two-storey version of the "tower," or *lou ge*, at Longjing near Hangzhou. Note that it is in fact built against a hillside.

4 Studies [*shu fang*]

When siting a study in a garden you should not strictly separate inside and outside, but should choose a secluded site and give easy access to and from the garden; yet this should be done in such a way that people strolling in the garden will be unaware of its existence. No matter whether the internal construction is that of a studio, guest lodging, living-room or private apartment, you should make use of the scenery outside, so that its placement seems natural and elegant and it is deeply imbued with the flavor of mountains and forests. If it is to be a separate building, first consider the shape of space available for the foundations: whether they are to be square, round, long, flat, wide, expansive, curved, or narrow, the effect should be like that of the extra half span of the great hall mentioned above, naturally secluded. Whether a tower or a single-storey building, a covered walkway or a gazebo, its form should be in accordance with the shape of the foundations, and the building should fit in with the lie of the land.

5 Pavilions [*ting xie*]

A shady gazebo among the flowers, a quiet pavilion on the edge of the water—these are the quintessence of garden design. But why should gazebos only be built among flowers, or pavilions only beside water? What about bamboo groves around a spring, hill-tops with a fine view, slopes thickly covered with jade bamboo, or cliffs with gnarled and dark-green pine? If you build over a stream as if over the rivers Hao or Pu, you will feel as though you are watching the fish with Master Zhuang;[83] or if you support the building

48 A gateway in alignment with the main building to which it leads; in this case the building is of the type known as a *ge*. Hu Pao Si, Hangzhou.

on stilts in the water as if it was above the waves of the Canglang, you can wash your feet—and not just in the old song.[84] There is no set formula for pavilions, nor any rule for their layout.

6 Covered Walkways [*lang fang*]

Before laying the foundations of a covered walkway, first make sure you reserve enough space around it. You may keep the space for it before or behind a particular building, from which it may lead to the heart of a wood.

51 Covered walkway, Yi Yuan (Elegant Garden), Nanxiang.

It may ascend half way up a mountain or go right down to the water's edge, following the rise and fall, the twisting and turning of the ground, stopping and starting, curving and bending in a natural way. No garden should lack this particular feature.

7 Artificial Mountains [*jia shan*]

Generally speaking, the foundations of most artificial mountains should be laid close to water. You must first estimate the finished height of the peak before you can decide the depth of the foundations. You must remember that the piled up rocks will affect the sky-line, and the surrounding earth will

49 (facing page top) Pavilion on a hill-top, Ge Yuan.

50 (facing page bottom) Pavilion surrounded by water and used for theatrical performance, He Yuan.

53 (above right) Artificial mountain in unusually close proximity to a building, Ge Yuan.

take up space on the ground, so you should avoid setting them among your dwelling-houses; it is preferable for them to be widely spread around.

III BUILDINGS

All family seats and dwelling-houses, whether of five spans or three, should be built in accordance with the accepted conventions. Only studios set in gardens, whether a standard span in size or half a span, are most exquisite when built to take advantage of the seasonal scenery.

The orientation should be in accordance with the lie of the land, and the master-mason and landowner should be in agreement on the design. Family dwelling-houses are bound to be subject to general discussion, but the outlying buildings will only be right if they harmonize with the landscape.

Although all the main halls will be generally similar, those which are near terraces and gazebos should have something special in their design. In the front you should add retractable awnings, and at the back extend the eaves to form a verandah. There must be a main beam which can support a superstructure. In the construction you must arrange high and low properly, and build the left and right sides separately.

You should absolutely avoid building a pair of side rooms under the eaves of the main hall, for fear of narrowing the courtyard area. If you add an extra roof extension over the steps, you should make the steps themselves wider from front to back.

You should not allow any carving on the short posts between beams and roof timbers, and why should you have to follow the convention of having the door jamb supports carved into the shape of drums? You should always follow what is elegant and simple, and take what is most orthodox and straightforward from ancient times. Colored painting may look handsome, but you are just adding blue and green to the natural color of the wood. It is all too easy for carving to look vulgar if you add decorative fairies and birds carved in relief.

In the case of a single long and winding covered walkway, when you begin to set up the pillars you should pay attention to the magical effects of

54 "At the back extend the eaves to form a verandah." Back of the building known as Hu Tian Zi Chun, Ge Yuan.

55 View of ordinary living quarters, Shen Yuan, Shaoxing.

changes in viewpoint. In the case of several small buildings dotted about, you should thoroughly consider the exact placing of doorways, and deliberate whether their design is precisely right.

Interesting pavilions and finely wrought gazebos should be built here and there among brightly colored flowers; many-storeyed towers and lofty buildings should rear up above the clouds. Different prospects will appear and disappear inexhaustibly; an unending springtime will hover about your garden. Clouds will drift by beyond your threshold; water will flow through the mirror of your pool. The colors of the hills cannot be washed away, and the cries of cranes are wafted to your ears.

The whole area, a natural work of art, will resemble Yinghu, the land of the Immortals. You can fully satisfy your craving for woods and springs, and rejoice abundantly in the surroundings of parks and gardens.

56 "Lofty buildings rear above the clouds." Yi Yuan.

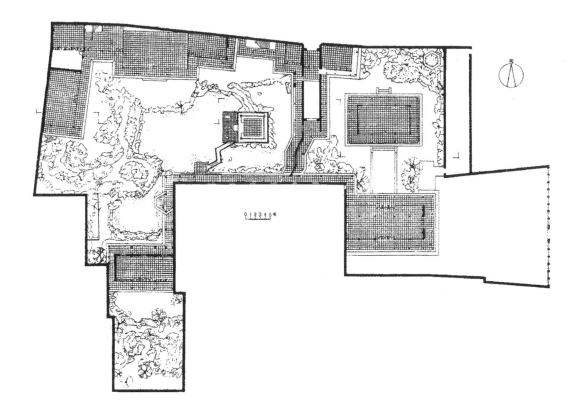

57 Plan of He Yuan (from Chen Congzhou, *Yangzhou Yuanlin*). Note the contrast between the more formal buildings of 3 and 5 spans to the east, and the more irregularly shaped buildings in the garden proper to the west.

If you can act according to these principles, your garden will be worthy to last for a thousand years.

Thus your hall will be a magnet for cultured men and your pavilion will have the reputation of another Cao Xuan.[85] You may be unable to compete with buildings created by Lu Yun, but you will be able to wield your axe outside Lu Ban's door.[86]

You must search out the unconventional and make sure it is in accord with your own wishes. The trite and conventional should be totally eliminated.

1 Gate Towers [*men lou*]

Raising a tower above the gate gives an imposing effect, like the towers rising above the battlements of a city-wall. However, gates without towers may also be referred to as "gate towers."

2 Halls [*tang*]

What the ancients referred to as "halls" were buildings of which the front half had been cleared out to form an audience hall. The word "hall" [*tang*] means "imposing" [*dang*]. That is to say, the hall is the main central building facing south, which thus carries the implication of "splendid [*tang-tang*] and conspicuous."

3 Chapels [*zhai*]

The difference between a chapel[87] and a hall is that the placing of a chapel is particularly secluded and its atmosphere restrained; it has the power to make

58 Gateway, Zhenjiang.

60 Staircase to private apartments, He Yuan.

people feel a sense of holy awe. This means creating a place of retreat where the spirit can be nourished, so it is not suitable for the design to be too open.

4 Living-rooms [*shi*]

The ancients said the rear half of a building should be furnished to make a living-room. The *Book of Shang* mentions "earthen rooms." The *Zuo Chronicle* mentions cave dwellings. The phrase "Turning rooms, winding and remote" recorded in the *Selection of Literature* indicates "curved rooms."[88]

5 Chambers [*fang*]

The *Explanation of Names* states: "A chamber is a protection." As such rooms protect privacy and divide inner from outer they are used as bedchambers.[89]

6 Lodgings [*guan*]

A place where travelers put up temporarily is known as a lodging, and the word can also be used to mean an alternative dwelling-place. Nowadays, studies are also referred to as "lodgings," and guest apartments, or rooms for travellers, are called "borrowed lodgings."

59 Gourd gateway, Shou Xi Hu, Yangzhou. Note the decorative features of the wall as well as the gateway itself.

7 Towers [*lou*]

The *Analytical Dictionary of Characters* states: "A building of more than one storey is known as a tower." The *Er Ya* states: "That which is narrow and built with curves is a tower."[90] This means that the windows are open, not papered or latticed, and all the window spaces are arranged regularly. The construction design is simply a hall with extra storeys above it.[91]

8 Terraces [*tai*]

The *Explanation of Names* states: "The word 'terrace' means 'support.' That is to say, earth is built up so that it is both firm and high and can provide adequate support." Terraces in gardens may be made from rocks piled up high with a flat surface; or they may be constructed of flat planks laid on a high wooden framework, with no buildings on top; or an extensive open step may stretch out in front of a tall building—all these are types of terrace.

9 Belvederes [*ge*]

A belvedere is a building with a roof sloping in four directions and windows on all four sides. The Unicorn Building in the Han dynasty, the Lingyan Building in the Tang dynasty and so on were all of this design.[92]

63 The building to be seen among trees in the background is a *ge* (Zhenjiang). See also plate 48.

61 (facing page top) "Interesting pavilions… among brightly colored flowers." Ge Yuan.

62 (facing page bottom) The larger building is the Yi Yu Xuan (Gallery of Seemly Rain) in the Ge Yuan.

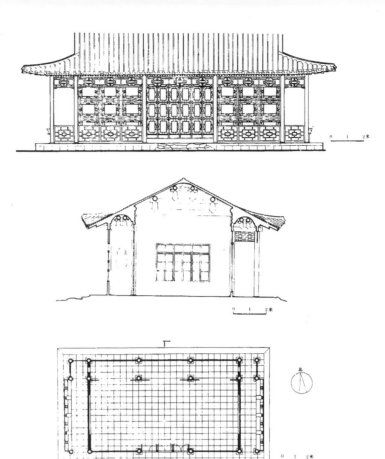

64 Elevation, section and plan of the Gallery of Seemly Rain (from Chen Congzhou, *Yangzhou Yuanlin*). Note the unusual windows in the end walls, and the arched structure of the verandahs, which is the "vaulting" referred to in section 13.

10 Pavilions [*ting*]

The *Explanation of Names* states: "The word 'pavilion [*ting*]' means 'to stop [*ting*].' It is a place for travelers to stop and rest." Sikong Tu's Xiu Xiu [Rest Rest] Pavilion was named for this meaning.[93] There is no fixed design for pavilions: they may be three-cornered, four-cornered, five-cornered, plum-flower shaped, six-cornered, rectangular with one curved side,[94] eight-cornered, or cruciform, according to your wishes and to what is appropriate to their situation. Only a plan can give some indication of the design of any particular pavilion.

11 Gazebos [*xie*]

The *Explanation of Names* states: "The word '*xie* [gazebo]' means 'to borrow [*jie*].'" Gazebos are made to "borrow" or take advantage of the scenery. They may be sited beside water or among flower-beds, and may also have a variety of structures.

12 Galleries [*xuan*]

The form of a gallery is similar to that of a carriage, and the word has the implication of "spacious and lofty," so it is most suitable to site a gallery in a high open place where it can perform its proper function of enhancing the scenery.[95]

13 Vaulting [*juan*]

Vaulting is added on in front of the main hall if you wish to increase the appearance of spaciousness; or if you want to have a small building with a roof shaped other than an inverted V, you may also use this design. But it can only be used with the structure of a four-cornered pavilion or a gallery.

14 Penthouses [*yan*]

The ancients said: a house built up against a cliff face is called a penthouse. Buildings which are not complete in themselves but use a cliff face to form part of their structure are known as penthouses.

15 Covered Walkways [*lang*]

The covered walkway is a further development of the verandah. For it to be a proper walkway it should be both winding and long. In ancient times so-called "winding walkways" turned at right angles like a carpenter's square. But the winding walkways which I build now bend like the letter S,[96] curving with the form of the ground and bending with the lie of the land. They may curl round the middle of a hill or run down to the water's edge, pass among flowers or cross a moat, endlessly twisting and turning. The Seal Cloud Walkway in the Wu Garden is of this type.[97] I have seen several spans of the Gaoxia Walkway in the Sweet Dew Temple at Zhenjiang; there is a tradition that it was built by Lu Ban.[98]

16 Five-pillared Structures [*wu jia liang*]

A five-pillared structure, in the case of a main hall, requires the use of a weight-bearing beam. If an extra upright is added at the front and at the back, the arrangement will be that of a seven-pillared structure. If vaulting is added in the front, it is essential to add a superstructure to make it high and spacious, otherwise the front eaves will come down very low and the result will be a very dark interior. If you want the building to be more extensive, you can also add a walkway in front. A smaller five-pillared structure can be used to construct pavilions, gazebos or libraries. If you replace the rear "baby pillar" with a full-length pillar, you can attach a screen door to divide the front from the rear, or alternatively you can equally well add a walkway.

17 Seven-pillared Structures [*qi jia liang*]

A seven-pillared structure is the standard structure for one-storey

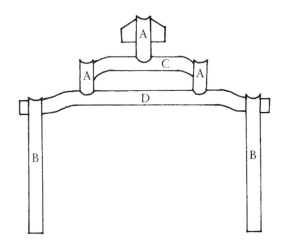

A "baby" pillars
B visible pillars
C minor weight-bearing beam
D major weight-bearing beam

Diag. iii.1: Five-pillared cross-beam design
Vaulting may be added in front and another upright at the back: this forms a design the same as the seven-pillared structure.

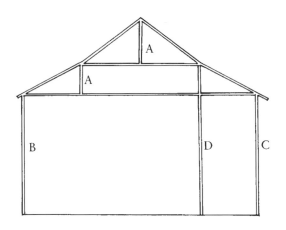

A "baby" pillars
B front walkway pillar
C rear walkway pillar
D If this "baby" pillar is changed for a full-length pillar you should make screen doors.

Diag. iii.2: Small five-pillared design
Whenever you are building a study, a small chapel or a pavilion, this design can be used to divide it into front and rear rooms.

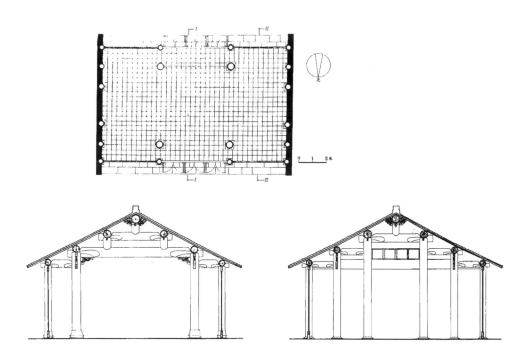

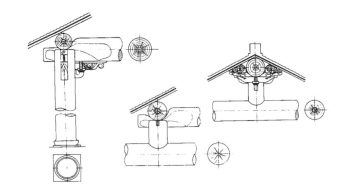

65 Seven-pillared structure: plan and cross-sections of hall in Mao family residence, Great East Gate Street, Yangzhou (from Chen Congzhou, *Yangzhou Yuanlin*). Note that although this is a seven-pillared structure there are only six full-length pillars in section as the "backbone pillars" have been omitted, leaving only a "baby pillar" under the roof ridge.

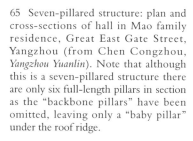

buildings in general. If vaulting is used in front of the hall, you should also use a "rough-frame" superstructure. If you add one pillar in front and behind, this makes a variation of the nine-pillared structure. If you are constructing a building of several storeys, you should first count how many rows of eaves there will be from top to bottom and then calculate the required length of the pillars; you can also add short cross-beams half way up if the timbers are not long enough for a single pillar.

18 Nine-pillared Structures [*jiu jia liang*]

In buildings of the nine-pillared structure, the skill lies in putting them together. Four, five or six spans may be linked, and they may face north, south, east or west. Alternatively, they may be separated into rooms of three spans two spans, one span or half a span, and the front divided from the back. You need to use a diagonal supporting beam in such a way that the viewer cannot see its position. Or you may add another storey on top. There are all kinds of subtleties which cannot all be shown in diagrams; you just have to use whatever structure is appropriate to the particular circumstances, and not confine yourself to a single design.

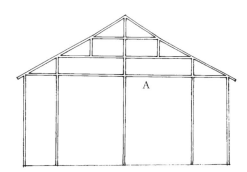

A The joist should be used; it is convenient to decorate.

Diag. III.3: Design of seven-pillared structure The seven-pillared structure is standard for buildings in general.

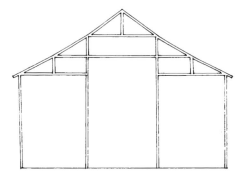

Diag. III.4: Seven-pillared "pickle" structure[99] Not to use the central line of "backbone" pillars clears the way for hanging paintings;[100] in this way, also, if the building as a whole is oriented north-south, the side rooms can open to the east and west.[101]

A diagonal rafter
B room division
C walkway pillar

Diags. III.5 – 7: Nine-pillared structures This type of structure is suitable for division into several rooms, and the divisions can be freely positioned. You may use "watersheds" (diagonal rafters) and the rooms can open to the north, south, east or west as you please.

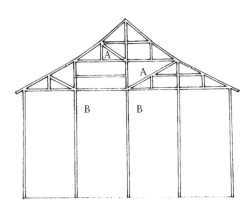

III.5 With five full-length pillars

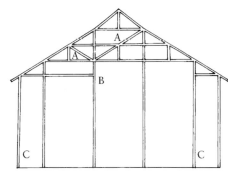

III.6 With six full-length pillars

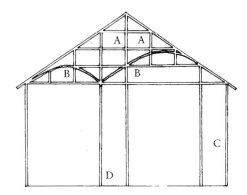

A "rough-frame" superstructure
B vaulting
C walkway pillar
D room division
III.7 With vaulting at front and rear

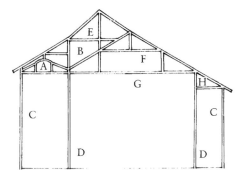

Diag. III.8: "Rough-frame" superstructure Only when adding vaulting in front of a main hall do you need to use a "rough-frame" superstructure, and you may also add a walkway in the front which may have moulded corners.

A front vaulting
B main rafter
C walkway pillar
D visible pillar
E "rough-frame" superstructure
F minor weight-bearing beam
G five-pillar weight-bearing beam
H rear structure

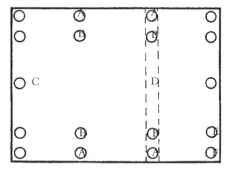

Diag. III.9: Ground plan When starting any building you should always draw a plan of it first. Site the pillars and place the plinths, measure the width of the foundations, and only then draw an elevation. In a main hall the central span ought to be larger and the side spans smaller; they must not be of equal size.

Seven-pillared structure, with five full-length pillars

A walkway pillars
B "lapel" pillars
C backbone pillars
D five-upright weight-bearing beam
E ranking beam
F ranking walkway pillar

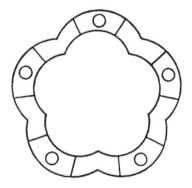

Diag. III.10: Ground plan of plum-flower shaped pavilion First lay out stones to form a plum-flower shaped foundation, then set up pillars on the tips of the petals, and build up to the roof-top, joining the eaves; it will look just like a plum-flower.

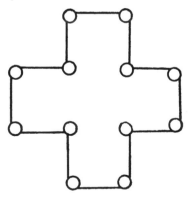

Diag. III.11: Ground plan of cruciform pavilion Twelve pillars are set up in groups of four, the roof rises from a square to a point, and the eaves all round also form a cross. I will not give designs for any types of pavilion other than the plum-flower and cruciform shapes. Since these have never before been built, I give a rough idea of them from the ground plan. These two types of pavilion can only be roofed with thatch.[103]

19 The "Rough-frame" Superstructure [*cao jia*]

Use of the "rough-frame" is essential for great halls. On any building where vaulting is added and a gutter would be needed between the two roof slopes, the vaulting is both troublesome to construct and not at all durable, so the "rough-frame" superstructure is used to create a tidy appearance. If this faces to the front of the building, we describe the building as a hall, if to the rear, a tower; this is the secret of using the "rough-frame," of which you cannot afford to be ignorant.

20 The Main Rafter [*zhong chuan*]

The main rafter is the rafter on which the "rough-frame" is constructed; it forms a "false room" within the building. In any building which is divided so that you cannot see the roof, the use of a main rafter with diagonal rafters is aesthetically preferable. Wherever a walkway is directly attached to a building, or there is a structure built up against the wall in such a way that the roofline runs straight down, use of the main rafter is essential.

21 Moulded Roof Corners [*mo jiao*]

"Moulded" roof corners are the same as the "drawn-up" roof corners of high buildings.[102] They are an essential part of buildings which are open on all four sides, and of all pavilions. From three-cornered to eight-cornered pavilions, all have their own type of moulding or up-turning, which cannot all be described here; each designer has his own preferred style. If you add a walkway in front of a main hall, you can also give it moulded corners, but you will have to decide the amount of upturning which is suitable.

22 Ground Plans [*di tu*]

In general, masons can only draw an elevation showing the outward appearance of a building; it is unusual for one to be able to draw a ground plan. The ground plan constitutes the agreement between owner and builder. Supposing you want to build a single dwelling of several rooms' depth from front to back, you can use a ground plan to design it in advance. You can decide how many spans each room should comprise, and how many pillars should be used, and only then, when the design is complete, draw an elevation to show the finished building. If you want to build a more sophisticated building, using this technique first will make it easier to achieve.

IV NON-STRUCTURAL FEATURES

In all building the most difficult aspect is that of the non-structural features or decorative elements; moreover, buildings in gardens are different from ordinary dwelling-houses, for they must have order in variety and yet their orderliness must not be too rigid: even this orderliness should have a pleasing unpredictability, and yet at their most diverse there should be an underlying consistency. The distance between each building should be appropriate and their interrelationship ingeniously devised. The inner walls should be arranged symmetrically and separate doors should be constructed for entering and leaving. If the whole building has several spans, these can be divided or interconnected internally as you see fit. Why insist on keeping the corridor at the rear, looking as if it were tacked on superfluously?

    You may follow a path to some secluded spot, and there come upon yet another little cottage. Brick walls should keep a lane running between them, so that rooms and walkways can be connected together and not isolated. Wooden walls should have many window-openings so that one can secretly enjoy looking through them into different worlds, as if in a magic flask.[104] Pavilions and terraces should be visible through a crack, while towers and tall buildings should be surrounded by empty space. Where you think there is nothing more to see, the scenery should suddenly open out, and low-lying areas should unexpectedly slope upwards. Staircases should be built only at the sides of rooms, but steps may run up a hillside. Door leaves should not be other than conventional, but window lattices may change according to

66 "Order in variety." Yi Yuan, Nanxiang. Note the interplay of the different shapes of windows and doors. The calligraphy "*hui yue*" (painting the moon) above the moon-door is by Professor Chen Congzhou, who was involved in the restoration of the garden.

67 Covered walkway alongside a building, Ge Yuan, Yangzhou.

68 "Window opening on to a different world." Zhan Yuan, Nanjing.

68 "Window opening on to a different world." Zhan Yuan, Nanjing.

69 (facing page) "At their most diverse there should be an underlying consistency." He Yuan. Note the differing yet harmonious patterns of balustrades, cornice, window and paving.

fashion. When doors and windows are shut they should close tightly without a hair's breadth between them. Beside where you usually walk you should fix a balustrade or, even better, construct a covered walkway.

The insertion of a window half way up the wall is suitable for all rooms. In the old days windows in the shape of the seven-pointed water-caltrop flower were considered most artistic,[105] but nowadays those in the shape of willow leaves are most admired. If you glaze the window with panes of translucent shell, this will make it stronger, and if you add shutters on the outside this will give a greater feeling of security. In a building which is partly of one storey and partly of several, there is nothing to stop you fitting a ceiling of a single color attached to the cross-beams in the pillars. And in a hidden room or upper storey you might consider adding a semicircular moon window under the false eaves. When using a construction which involves high eaves, you should remember to use vaulting beneath them. If you hang up a cloth screen as a room-divider, it is as if you were creating a separate courtyard, while if two spaces share a common wall, passing through it feels like entering a hidden place of meditation.

To sum up, the construction of your buildings should be in accordance with the spirit of the times, while their appearance should elicit the appreciation of the most cultivated visitors.

1 Screen Doors

These are arranged symmetrically within the hall like a screen. The ancients sometimes used only one face, but nowadays it is standard practice to make doors with the two sides identical, and this is what is known as a "drum door."[106]

2 "Dust Supports"

"Dust support" is the ancient name for a ceiling. If too many birds and flowers are painted in the chessboard-like coffering, this is somewhat vulgar. The best treatments are either to make the ceiling completely flat, or paint it with wood-graining, or cover it with cotton cloth, or paper it. On the ground floor especially, you cannot omit fitting a ceiling.

3 Windows

In ancient times, most windows were the shape of water-caltrop flowers, in a square opening.[107] Later, people simplified them to a willow-leaf shape, and this is what became commonly known as a "never-ending window."[108] This style is quite elegant; I used it, varying the proportions and with many different patterns, but always maintaining its elegance, and deliberately keeping to the willow-leaf design. Some people use a balustrade pattern, set vertically, as a window; but for one thing this is too open, and also there is

70 (facing page) Circular door of cracked-ice pattern, as recommended for shutters, Ge Yuan.

nothing special to savor about it. It is best when the spaces of the lattice-work are just about one inch wide.[109] If they are any wider the effect is that of a balustrade or shutter and is to be avoided, so I have placed the diagrams for these later.

4 Shutters

Shutters are a protection outside the lattice-work of a window, and should be loosely spaced, wide and not too elaborate. They may take the form of a horizontal half-shutter or two flaps, for ease of opening and closing. Their pattern should be like that of a balustrade, or possibly even simpler. In a study they are known as "calligraphic windows," in the women's quarters as "embroidered windows."[110]

73 Underside of pavilion roof, Qiu Xia Pu. The clerestory here serves the same function as that presumably served by the moon window under false eaves to which Ji Cheng refers.

72 (facing page) Second storey walkway, Ge Yuan. Note the window lattices and the shape of the door on the right.

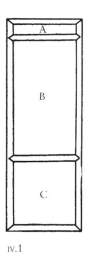
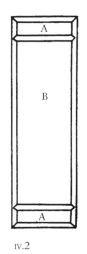

A belt
B gap for lattice-work
C board

Diag. ɪv. 1: Pattern for tall windows In ancient times windows were divided between open lattice-work and solid board in the proportion of four to six; the windows therefore did not admit much light. The modern method is for the open lattice-work to occupy seven- or eight-tenths of the window space and the board only two- or three-tenths. To estimate the height of the window, it should be about the height of a table; if higher, then no more than four or five *cun*s higher at the most.

Diag. ɪv.2: Pattern for low windows In ancient times the division in low windows between open lattice-work and solid board was the same as in tall windows, so they let in even less light. The modern method is to use a "belt" at both top and bottom, filled in either with a board or with lattice-work.

ɪv.1

ɪv.2

Diags. ɪv.3 – 45: Patterns for Lattice-work Nowadays willow-leaf patterned window are preferred as they are both spacious and simple. The pattern can be changed according to the shape of the window and you can use whatever pattern you want.

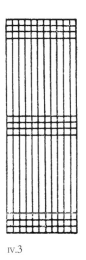
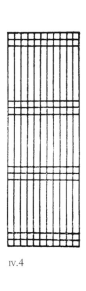
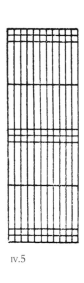

Diags. ɪv.3 – 12: Willow-leaf patterns I – 10

I

ɪv.3

ɪv.4

ɪv.5

ɪv.6

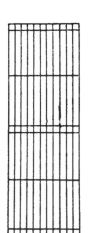

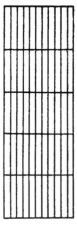

ɪv.7

ɪv.8

ɪv.9

ɪv.10

ɪv.11

ɪv.12

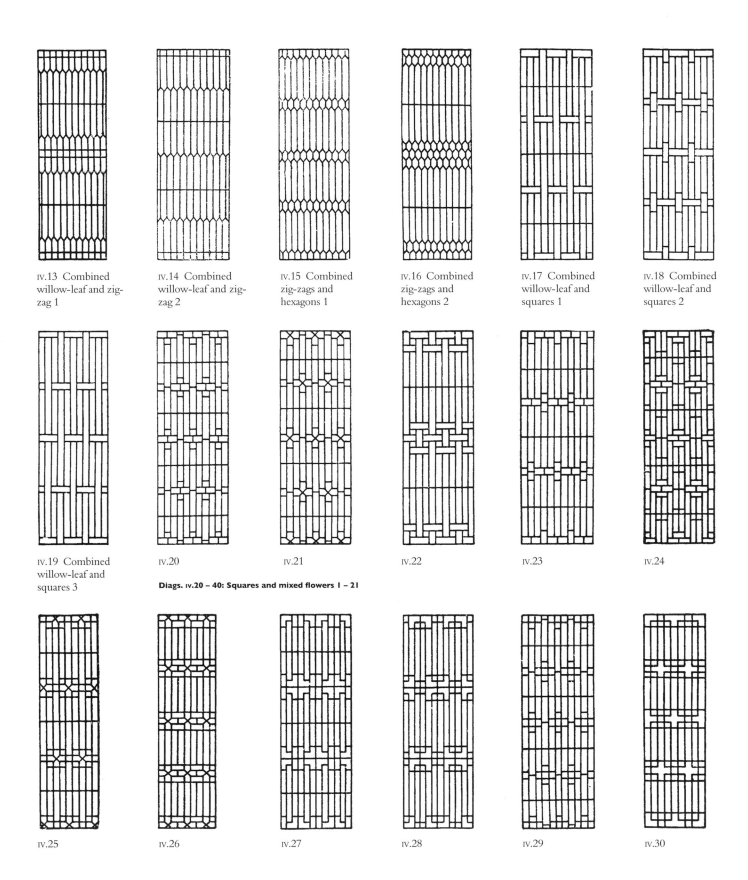

IV.13 Combined willow-leaf and zig-zag 1

IV.14 Combined willow-leaf and zig-zag 2

IV.15 Combined zig-zags and hexagons 1

IV.16 Combined zig-zags and hexagons 2

IV.17 Combined willow-leaf and squares 1

IV.18 Combined willow-leaf and squares 2

IV.19 Combined willow-leaf and squares 3

IV.20

IV.21

IV.22

IV.23

IV.24

Diags. IV.20 – 40: Squares and mixed flowers 1 – 21

IV.25

IV.26

IV.27

IV.28

IV.29

IV.30

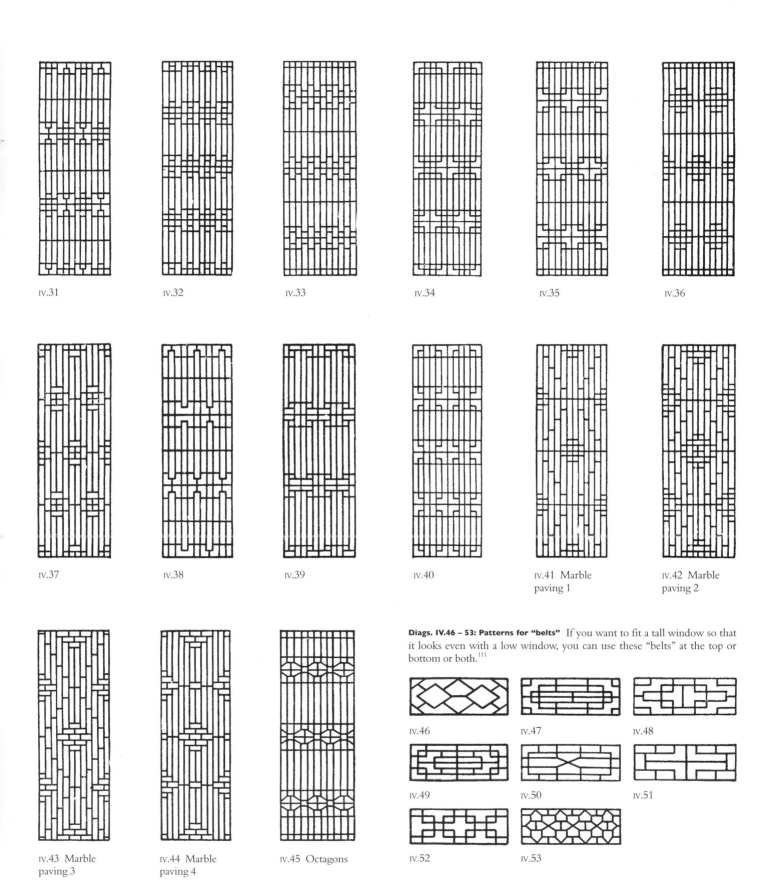

IV.31

IV.32

IV.33

IV.34

IV.35

IV.36

IV.37

IV.38

IV.39

IV.40

IV.41 Marble paving 1

IV.42 Marble paving 2

IV.43 Marble paving 3

IV.44 Marble paving 4

IV.45 Octagons

Diags. IV.46 – 53: Patterns for "belts" If you want to fit a tall window so that it looks even with a low window, you can use these "belts" at the top or bottom or both.[111]

IV.46

IV.47

IV.48

IV.49

IV.50

IV.51

IV.52

IV.53

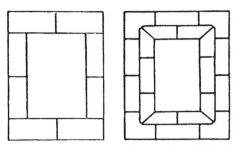

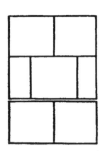

Diags. IV.54-55: Shutters Shutters should be of loosely-spaced design; they should either have paper pasted over the spaces or thin silk between the wood, or be painted. You may use some less decorative lattice-work. Or you may choose, from the patterns for balustrades, a pattern that is loosely spaced and not elaborate, and is also sturdy in use.

Diag. IV.56: Cracked ice pattern The cracked ice pattern is the most suitable for shutters.[112] The pattern of it is both simple and elegant; you may vary the design as you please. The subtlety of it is that it can be more widely spaced at the top and denser at the bottom.[113]

Diag. IV.57: Bipartite type There is no restriction on the design of a bipartite shutter, but it is best if it appears to be a single leaf when closed .

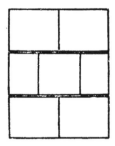

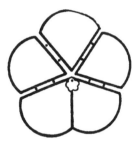

Diag. IV.58: Tripartite type The middle leaf should be attached to the upper leaf, so that when you open and prop up the upper leaf it does not take up too much space.[114] For joining the middle to the upper leaf, you should use a brass hinge.

Diag. IV.59: Plum-flower design In a plum-flower shutter, the petals should be made separately. You should use a plum-flower swivel in the middle for convenience of opening and closing.

Diag. IV.60: Opening plum-flower design Form two of the petals so that they are joined together and three of them separate. Fasten one point of the plum-flower swivel to the tip or upper part of the two joined petals. When the other three petals are in place, turn the swivel upwards and fix it in place.

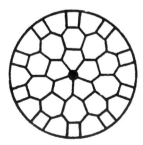

Diag. IV.61: Hexagonal design

Diag. IV.62: Round mirror design

74 Balustrade on second-storey walkway, He Yuan. Note also the pattern of the cornice below.

75 The decorative "balustrade" on the roof ridge (He Yuan) is formed of a stylised version of the character *shou* (longevity).

76 Doorway in Ge Yuan: the beds of bamboo are surrounded by a rustic "foot-high balustrade," itself made of bamboo. The character *ge* (个) in the garden's name is an allusion to the shape of a bamboo stem with leaves.

5 Balustrades

Balustrades should be designed very freely, and the simpler they are the more elegant they will be. The ancient patterns of concentric squares or swastikas should be completely rejected, or kept for occasional use on bamboo beds for summer or the plinths of Buddhist statues.[115] They absolutely must not be used for garden architecture. Over the course of years I have amassed one hundred different designs, some more complex and elaborate, some more simple and refined. The designs appear below in order of their development, for convenience of use, starting with designs based on the shape of a pen-shaft [a straight line]. Recently some people have made balustrades incorporating seal characters;[116] not only do the different numbers of strokes make an unbalanced design, but there is no connection in meaning between the different characters. As for my own collection of designs, I feel it is still far from comprehensive, and can certainly be refined and added to.

Diags. IV.63 – 123: Pen-shaft type We begin with balustrade designs based on the pen shaft, first single, then double; the double ones can be developed however you wish. These different designs are all symmetrically formed and they all have names. I was afraid the ones without names would be lost, so I have recorded them all in order. They include some which are not easy to put together, so in these cases I have also described how to construct them, to make things easier for the joiners.

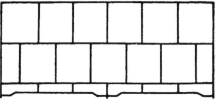

IV.63 Pen shaft

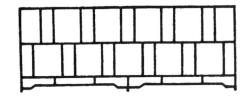

IV.64 Double pen shaft

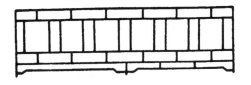

IV.65 Development of pen-shaft design 1

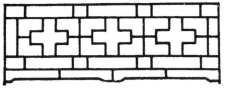

IV.66 Development of pen-shaft design 2

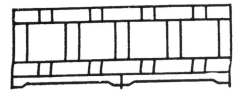

IV.67 Development of pen-shaft design 3

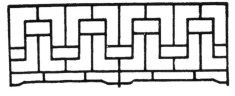

IV.68 Development of pen-shaft design 4

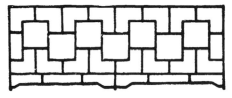

IV.69 Development of pen-shaft design 5

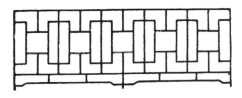

IV.70 Development of pen-shaft design 6

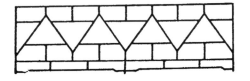

IV.71 Development of pen-shaft design 7

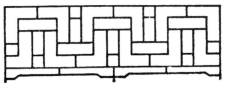

IV.72 Development of pen-shaft design 8

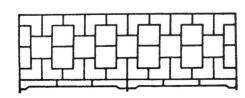

IV.73 Development of pen-shaft design 9

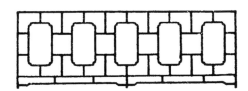

IV.74 Interlocking ribbon

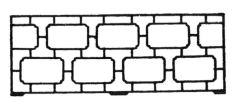

IV.75 Horizontal interlock 1

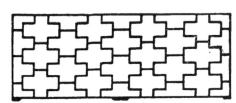

IV.76 Horizontal interlock 2

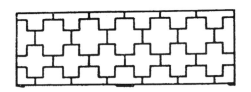

IV.77 Horizontal interlock 3

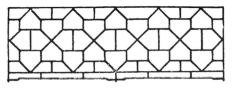

IV.78 Horizontal interlock 4

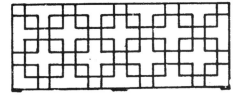

IV.79 Linked squares 1

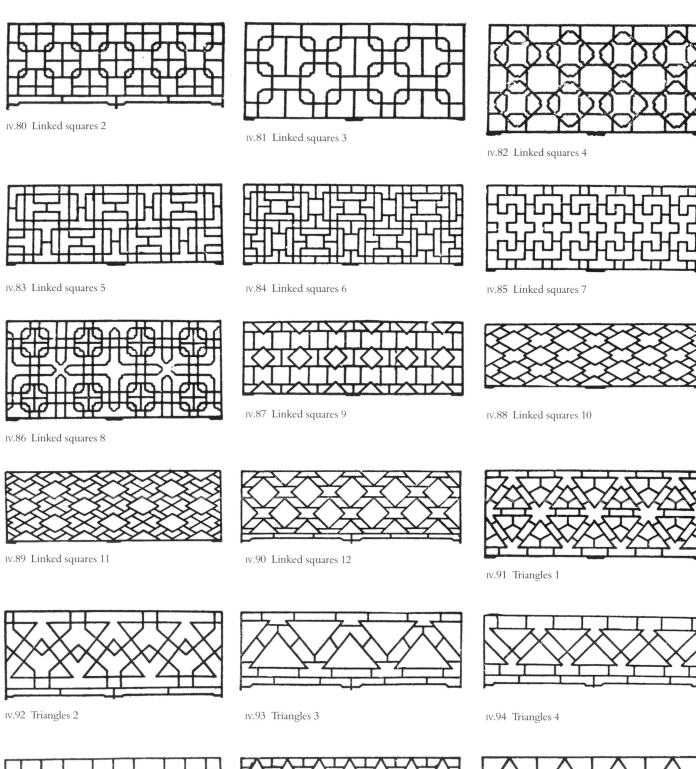

IV.80 Linked squares 2

IV.81 Linked squares 3

IV.82 Linked squares 4

IV.83 Linked squares 5

IV.84 Linked squares 6

IV.85 Linked squares 7

IV.86 Linked squares 8

IV.87 Linked squares 9

IV.88 Linked squares 10

IV.89 Linked squares 11

IV.90 Linked squares 12

IV.91 Triangles 1

IV.92 Triangles 2

IV.93 Triangles 3

IV.94 Triangles 4

IV.95 Triangles 5

IV.96 Triangles 6

IV.97 Triangles 7

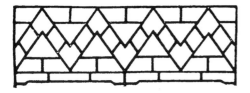

IV.98 Triangles 8

IV.99 Triangles 9

Diag. IV.100: Embroidered sunflower type First take six pieces of wood to form the heart of the flower, then add the petals, making it as shown in (1). (2) is one of the pieces forming the heart. Piece (3) forms the petals.

 1   2   3

IV.100

IV.101 Hexagons

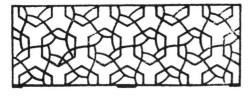

IV.102 Sunflowers 1

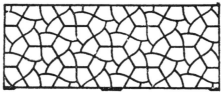

IV.103 Sunflowers 2

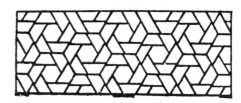

IV.104 Sunflowers 3

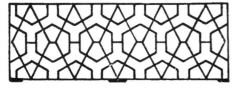

IV.105 Sunflowers 4

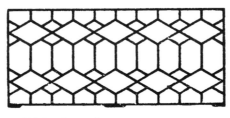

IV.106 Sunflowers 5

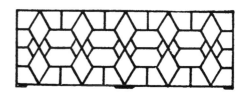

IV.107 Sunflowers 6

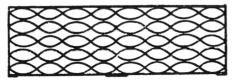

Diag. IV.108: Wave type This can be constructed using only this shape:

Diag. IV.109: Plum-flower type If you use pieces like this: you can simply fit them together to form the petals without drilling any holes.

IV.109

IV.110 Reflections 1

IV.111 Reflections 2

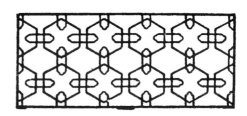

IV.112 Reflections 3

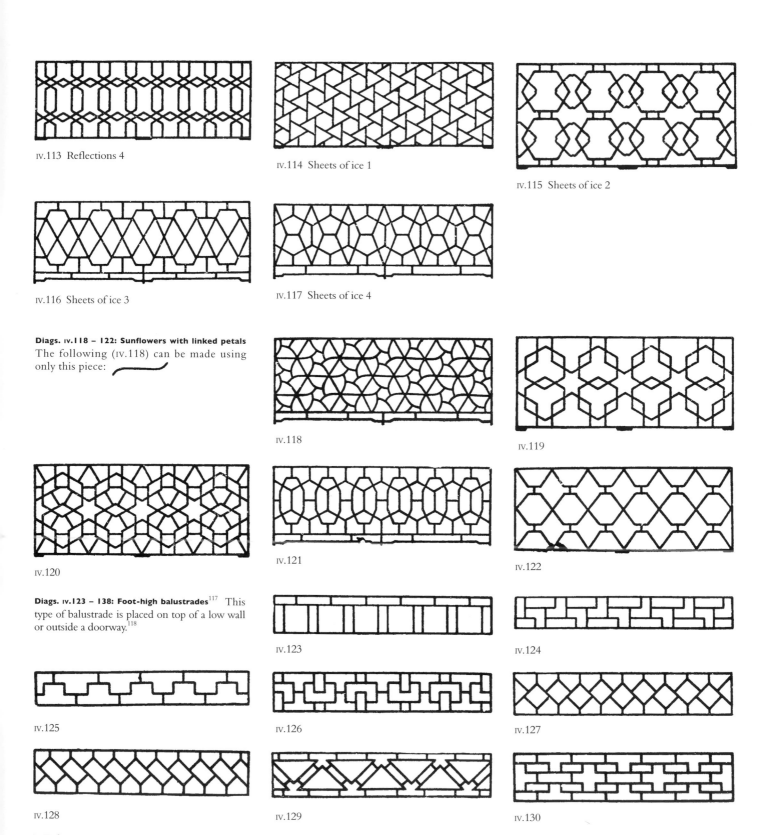

IV.113 Reflections 4

IV.114 Sheets of ice 1

IV.115 Sheets of ice 2

IV.116 Sheets of ice 3

IV.117 Sheets of ice 4

Diags. IV.118 – 122: Sunflowers with linked petals
The following (IV.118) can be made using only this piece:

IV.118

IV.119

IV.120

IV.121

IV.122

Diags. IV.123 – 138: Foot-high balustrades[117] This type of balustrade is placed on top of a low wall or outside a doorway.[118]

IV.123

IV.124

IV.125

IV.126

IV.127

IV.128

IV.129

IV.130

IV.131

IV.132

IV.133

IV.134

IV.135

IV.136

IV.137

IV.138

Diags. IV.139 – 155: Short balustrades

IV.139

IV.140

IV.141

IV.142

IV.143

IV.144

IV.145

IV.146

IV.147

IV.148

IV.149

IV.150

IV.151

IV.152

IV.153

IV.154

IV.155

Diags. IV.156 – 161: Short foot-high balustrades

IV.156

IV.157

IV.158

IV.159

IV.160

IV.161

IV.162

One hundred different designs of balustrade in total.

77 "The door should lead one on to the open spaces...." Qing Teng Shuwu (Green Vine Study), Shaoxing. Compare the shape of the door with the "long octagon" of diag. v. 5.

78 A classically simple moon-gate and a door with the "ruyi scepter" shape of diag. v. 9. Qing Teng Shuwu (Green Vine Study), Shaoxing.

79 A moon-gate flanked by "begonia" windows (diag. v. 26), Da Ming Temple, Yangzhou.

V STRUCTURAL FEATURES

1 Doorways

The style of moulding around the opening of a doorway should be chosen according to the current fashion. Not only can a doorway give a new look to a dwelling-house, it can make a garden look more elegant too. The fine work has to be done by a specialist mason, but the general arrangement needs to be directed by a person of discrimination, so that interesting thoughts can be aroused by a sudden vista, and inner feelings can be better expressed; thus, the fine silk window may be encircled with leaves of jade, and green buds peep from the soft willow-branches.[119] A mighty rock welcomes the visitor to a magical other world.[120] Fine bamboos play with their shadows, as if to the music of pan-pipes from over the water.[121] Grand views should be enjoyed, but the common world of dust can find no entry.

Absolutely avoid carving the door-jambs; the wall around a doorway should be polished smooth; everywhere the door should lead one on to the open spaces and in all directions draw one close to the scenery. If these matters were not handed down to posterity I fear they might be lost for ever, so I have assembled the following designs.

80 An elaborate form of plum-flower window, He Yuan (cf. diag. v. 24).

81 A door with the "octagon" shape of diag. v. 20. Da Ming Temple.

Diag. v.1: Square door with right-angled corners
Formerly, a square doorway made of polished brick could, if the craftsman wished, be made into an arched doorway, by putting a stone or wooden lintel on top of the bricks.[122] In making a square door nowadays, the wooden lintel is faced with polished brick tiles pinned on with wooden dowels, while dowels at a 45° angle are used to fix the mortized corners;[123] the effect is very elegant and attractive.

Diag. v.2: Arched doorway For all doorways made of polished bricks, you should decide the size of the bricks according to the thickness of the wall, and the inner side of the door-surround must use fully polished bricks. The outer edge of the surround must be no more than about an inch across and the bricks must be cut to fit, not moved around. Beyond the edge, the wall can be white-washed or faced with fully polished bricks.

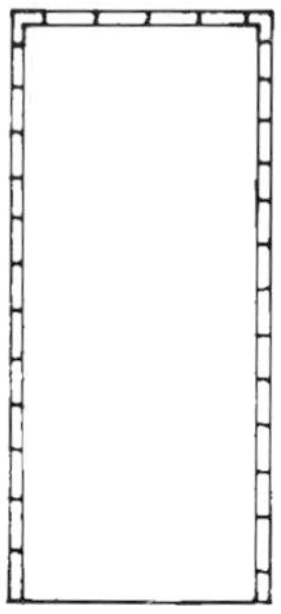

v.1

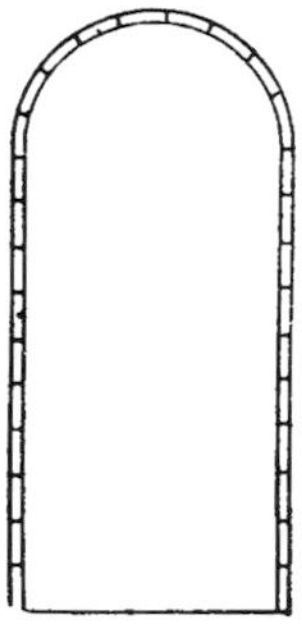

v.2

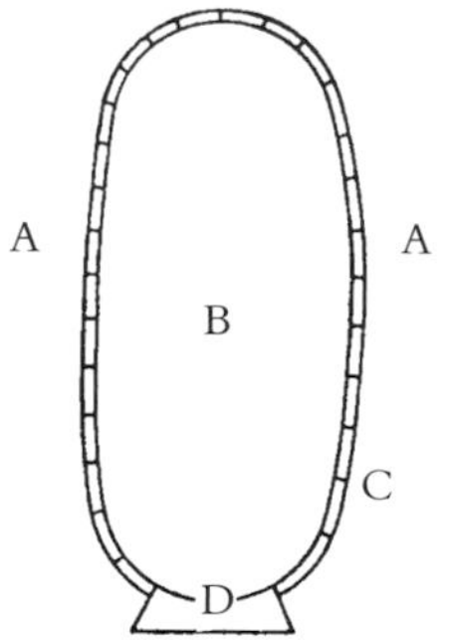

v.3 Arched and curved doorway
A whitewashed wall
B space
C all doorways use a "leather-strap" edge
D stone

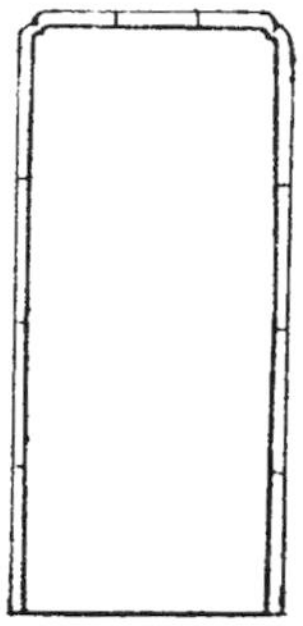

v.4 Turned-in corners

v.5 Long octagon

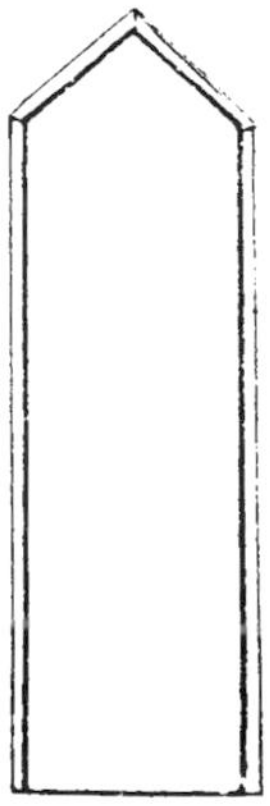

v.6 Pointed pentagon[124]

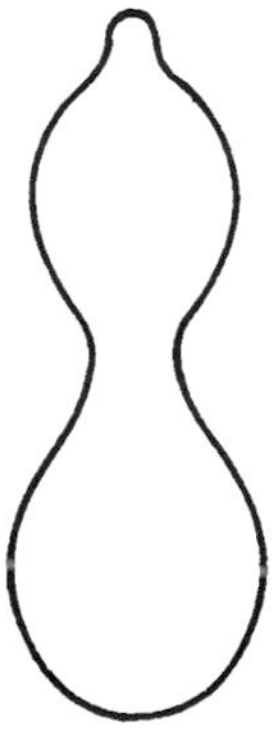

v.7 Gourd

Diags. v.8 – 10: These are suitable for use in a Buddhist shrine.

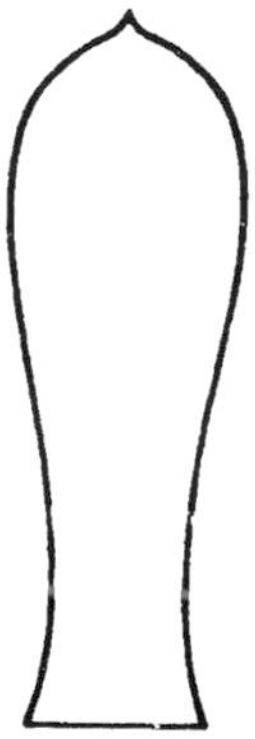

v.8 Lotus–petal

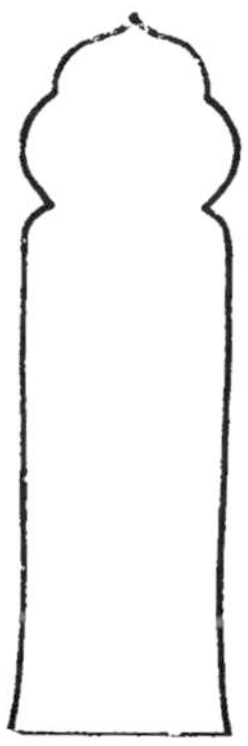

v.9 Ruyi scepter

v.10 Bodhi-leaf

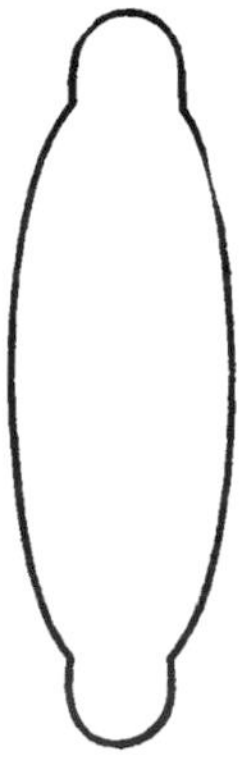

v.11 Sword guard

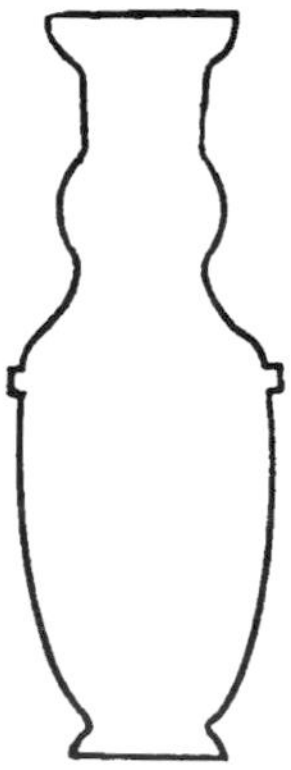

v.12 Han dynasty vase 1

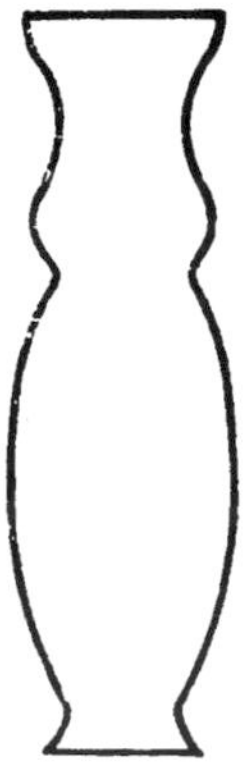

v.13 Han dynasty vase 2

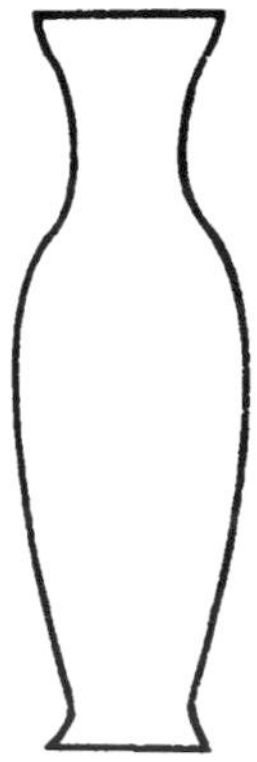

v.14 Han dynasty vase 3

v.15 Han dynasty vase 4

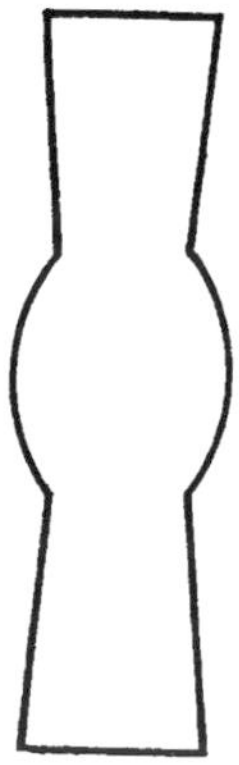

v.16 Decorative goblet

v.17 Vase for casting lots[126]

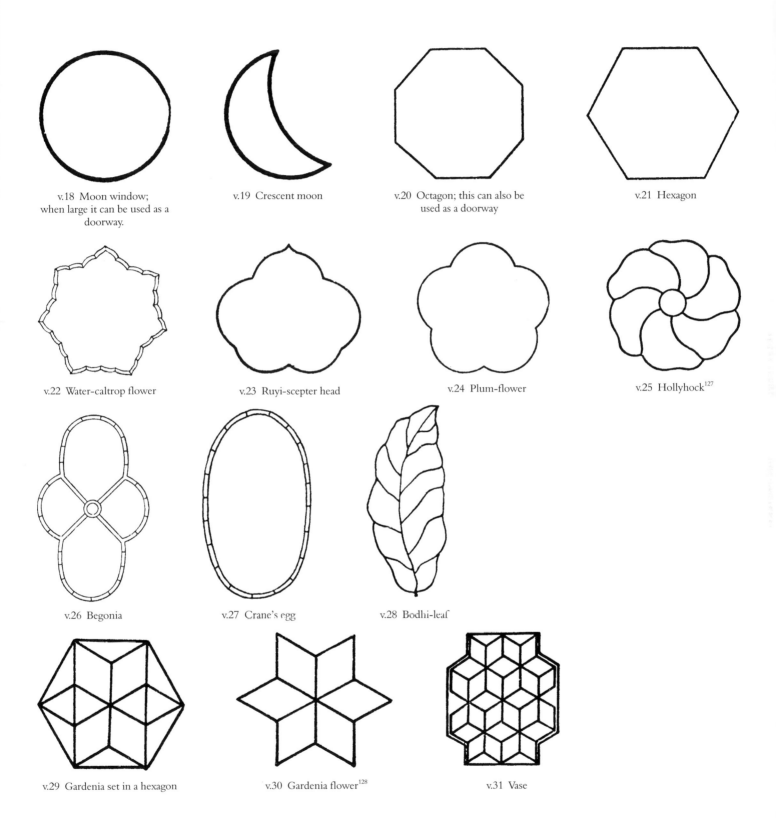

v.18 Moon window; when large it can be used as a doorway.

v.19 Crescent moon

v.20 Octagon; this can also be used as a doorway

v.21 Hexagon

v.22 Water-caltrop flower

v.23 Ruyi-scepter head

v.24 Plum-flower

v.25 Hollyhock[127]

v.26 Begonia

v.27 Crane's egg

v.28 Bodhi-leaf

v.29 Gardenia set in a hexagon

v.30 Gardenia flower[128]

v.31 Vase

2 Walls

Most surrounding walls for gardens are made of earth tamped between shuttering, or of blocks of stone, or take the form of thorny hedges. Now thorn hedges are better than flowering shrubs in that they look wilder and give the garden quite a flavor of the mountain forests. Walls within a garden, for example in front of a flowerbed or beside the water, along a path or around a hill, may be built perhaps of stone, or of brick, decorated with openwork or plain and polished; in fact they can be satisfactorily designed in many different ways. As long as they are elegant and contemporary, and worthy of appreciation, they will add to the beauty of your garden. Traditionally it has been considered that if a wall is decorated at the mason's pleasure with carvings of flowers, birds, fairies or monsters, this is really artistic; in fact not only is it ugly in a garden, it is unacceptable even in front of a dwelling-house. Sparrows build their nests among the carvings, which is most annoying; weeds accumulate all over them like creepers. Though you may try to drive the sparrows away you can never get rid of them; if you try to knock the weeds down, you risk damaging the wall. There is absolutely nothing you can do about the situation. Such decoration is the sort of thing that vulgar townees and stupid rustics go in for; the man of enlightened tastes will be more cautious.

When ordinary people build walls, if the ground is sloping or cramped, this limits their construction. But why not make the wall wider at one end than the other, in order to fit in with the regular proportions of the buildings?[129] This is something that neither masons nor landowners understand.

Whitewashed Walls. Traditionally, walls have been whitewashed with a mixture of paper-pulp and lime.[130] Those who like a fashionable look and want a glossy finish cover the wall with white wax and polish it up. Nowadays people use yellow sand from rivers and lakes, mix it with good quality lime and put on an undercoat; then they put on a top coat of more lime, brushing it lightly with a hemp brush, which makes it naturally so bright that you can see your reflection in it. If it gets dirty, the dirt can be washed off at once. This is known as a "mirror wall."

Decorative Brick Walls. Walls such as the screen wall inside a main gate or the wall facing a main hall can all use polished or square bricks laid with "hanging corners."[131] You may cut square bricks into octagons and intersperse them with smaller square bricks, or alternate small bricks with half bricks, and build up a brocade-like texture of "broken flowers." When you finish off the top, use several layers of square-shaped polished bricks to make "flying eaves."[132] You cannot use carved flowers, birds, fairies or monsters, as they seldom look artistic.

Openwork Brick Walls.[133] These may be built at any point where there is something worth looking at. They give the impression of guarding against what is without and concealing what is within. The old patterns built up from

82 An unusual example of a "wall within a garden…decorated with openwork." This one is a "two-storey" wall, with a door-way on the lower level and openwork "windows" on the upper. Zhenjiang.

83 Openwork wall with octagonal gate, Ge Yuan.

84 Screen wall inside the entrance to the Qiu Xia Pu, Jiading. As well as decorative carving which Ji Cheng might have disapproved of, this is decorated with bricks laid with "hanging corners." Note also the woven bamboo screens at either side, and the varieties of paving.

85 Openwork panel in wall, He Yuan. The geometric pattern provides a pleasing contrast with the natural forms of vegetation.

86 These open work panels give a glimpse through into another courtyard. Da Ming Temple.

87 "Precipitous mountain" built against a wall with open work panels above. He Yuan.

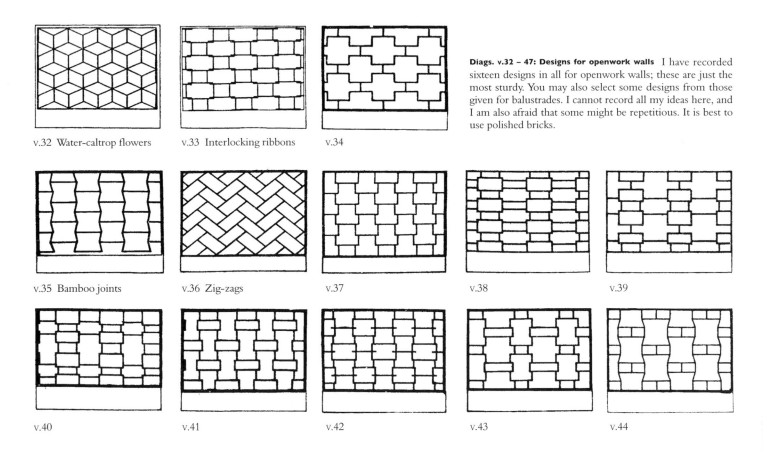

v.32 Water-caltrop flowers   v.33 Interlocking ribbons   v.34

v.35 Bamboo joints   v.36 Zig-zags   v.37   v.38   v.39

v.40   v.41   v.42   v.43   v.44

Diags. v.32 – 47: Designs for openwork walls I have recorded sixteen designs in all for openwork walls; these are just the most sturdy. You may also select some designs from those given for balustrades. I cannot record all my ideas here, and I am also afraid that some might be repetitious. It is best to use polished bricks.

tiles, such as "strings of cash," "heaped ingots" and "fish scales" should be avoided without exception.[134] I have sketched several other patterns below.

Unworked Stone Walls. All unworked stone can be built up into walls, but Huang rocks are the best.[135] Large stones should be separated by small ones. These walls are suitable for building among artificial mountains. If you use unworked dark stone you should use a mixture of lime and tung oil to fill in the gaps;[136] this style of construction is known as "cracked ice."[137]

3 Paving

Generally speaking, in laying paving or making a path, there is a slight difference between what pleases in gardens and in dwelling-houses. It is only in the midst of main halls and large buildings that you should pave the ground completely with polished bricks; a winding path or walk can be cobbled with various unworked stones of an oblong shape; in a central courtyard it may be appropriate to lay an interlocking zig-zag pattern; near steps you can also use a pattern of concentric squares.[138] If you intersperse octagons with squares, and select pebbles to set among them, you can obtain an effect like Sichuan brocade. The verandah outside a tall building, studded with flowers, will rival the glory of the Qin Terrace.[139] With a patterned fabric of tiles, and a terrace covered in stone slabs, you can sit on the ground and recite poetry to the flowers, or spread out a rug and raise your glass to the moon. Even shattered pieces of tile may come into their own: they can be chipped into shape and arranged in a rippling wave pattern, like stones on the floor of a lake. Even broken bricks may have their uses: they can be

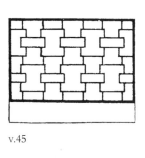

v.45

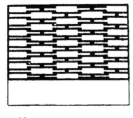

v.46

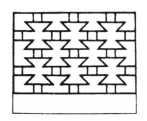

v.47

88   Laying paving in the traditional way, Jiading, 1985.

89   Begonia-patterned path through shrubbery, Yi Yuan, Nanxiang.

carved and fitted together around a plum-flower shape, in a random pattern like cracked ice. Walks and paths may be laid in a very conventional way, but steps should always be something out of the ordinary: lotuses seem to bloom under one's feet, as footsteps are heard all around.[140] As you pick up kingfisher feathers in the depths of the woods, a feeling of springtime arises from who knows where.[141]

A narrow way set around with flowers is better paved with stone, while an open courtyard surrounded by buildings should be laid with bricks. Paving of all kinds, square or round, should be laid in an appropriate way. Shaping the paving-stones should be the work of a specialist tiler, but unskilled labor may be used for the odd jobs.

Unworked Stone Walks. When laying walks in a garden, you should use

small stones of irregular shape, fitting them together like the seeds in a pomegranate; this is both hardwearing and elegant. A winding road running from high to low and leading from hill to valley can be given unity by this method. Some people set pebbles among the stones to make a pattern on the road; however, this is both not very durable and rather vulgar.

Pebbled Areas. Pebbles are suitable for laying on paths that are not frequently used. It is best if you can intersperse large stones with small, but I am afraid most workmen are incapable of this. It is also effective to use bricks or tiles, and inlay them to form various brocade-like patterns. But if you lay them in the form of cranes or deer or lions playing with a ball, and the lion ends up looking like a dog, it is just ridiculous.[142]

Crazy Paving.[143] Irregular "blue-slab" stones can be fitted together in "cracked ice" crazy paving. This is suitable for paths through a mountain gully or on a slope by the water, or before a terrace or beside a pavilion. The basic pattern can be seen above in my section on shutters, but you should be flexible in interpreting it and not be restricted in the way you lay the paving. It is particularly good if you can lay broken square bricks whose edges have been smoothed off.

Various Types of Brick Paving. Paving can be laid with various types of brick. Within a house, you should use shaped bricks, and lay them flat; in a courtyard, you should lay them on end. Square, repeated, or stepped interlocking zig-zag patterns were conventional in the old days. Modern patterns such as

90 Daoist *Yin-Yang* symbol with pebbles used for the *yang* part and tile-shards for the *yin*. Note also the tiles laid in a wave pattern in the foreground. Qiu Xia Pu, Jiading.

Diags. v.48 – 51: These four patterns are made with bricks set on edge.

v.48 Herringbone

v.49 Woven matting

Interlocking squares

Diags. v.52 – 59: These eight patterns make use of bricks studded with pebbles.

v.51 Woven-hat pattern

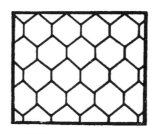

v.52 Hexagons

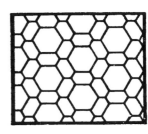

v.53 Grouped hexagons

v.54 Octagons interspersed with hexagons

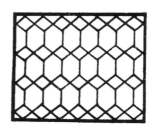

v.55 Overlapping hexagons

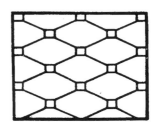

v.56 Elongated octagons

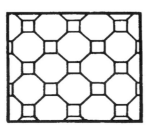

v.57 Octagons

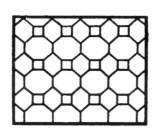

v.58 Begonia

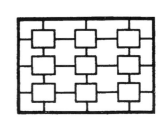

v.59 Squares interspersed with crosses

Diag. v.60: "Vanilla pod" edging Use a brick border and lay tiles in the vanilla pod pattern. The center can be paved either with bricks or with pebbles.

Diag. v.61: "Target" pattern[144] The combination of tiles with pebbles can be used only for this pattern.

Diag. v.62: "Wave" pattern Select thick and thin pieces of broken tile to lay this pattern; the top of the waves should use thick pieces and the sides thin.

v.60

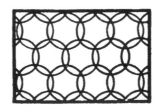

v.61

v.62

91 Decorative paving of pebbles and tile-shards in the form of a crane and pine-tree, symbols of long life. Ke Yuan.

92 Decorative paving of tile-shards in the form of a butterfly. Ou Yuan.

93 Decorative paving of pebbles and tile-shards, contrasting with raised stone paving. He Yuan.

herringbone, woven matting, or woven hat pattern are all possible provided the bricks are found in a suitable length.[145] See the accompanying patterns.

VI SCENIC FEATURES

1 Raising Mountains[146]

When starting to raise a mountain, first set up wooden posts, calculating the correct length and examining the firmness of the ground. According to what the ground requires, dig holes and set up pairs of pillars, then estimate the final height of the mountain and set up a block and tackle. All ropes should be fastened firmly so that any lifting can be done securely. Lay the base of the mountain with rough stones and use large pieces of stone to conceal completely the ends of the pillars. Fill your trench with rubble and mortar, and in wet places drive in the "bones" of the mountain as far as you can. Start by piling up large, solid rocks, and then gradually build up with smaller, jagged stones. So-called "thin" and "riddled" rocks are naturally impressive, while "filigree" rocks depend on being artistically positioned.[147]

The most vital aspect of a cliff is its perpendicularity; when constructing an overhanging brow, make sure the rear part is solidly built. Precipices, peaks, caves and gullies should look as if they were boundless, and streams, valleys, slopes and promontories should be as majestic as the real thing. As you wander wherever your feet take you, you may doubt that there is any boundary to the place; as you raise your head to gaze around, deep emotions will be stirred in you. The narrow paths should be long and winding; the lofty peaks should be glorious and venerable. The magnificent scenery on every side, the mountains and forests a hand's breadth away—their subtle attraction all springs from one man's imagination, and their elegance derives from a mere heap of earth.

If a single rock is set upright in the center as the "chief stone" and two more rocks, known as "split peaks," are inserted on each side, the single one will stand in solitary magnificence and the lesser ones will act as supporters; they will seem to be arranged in order of rank and will give the impression of waiting on command. Although you should generally avoid putting the "chief stone" in the exact center, this can be done if it seems right. Although it may be better on balance not to make use of "split peaks," if they are used, they must be used in a decisive way.

Too symmetrical an arrangement will look like the censer flanked by two vases on an altar, and a confused arrangement will look like the instruments of torture, the "hill of knives" or "tree of swords."[148] Such peaks will lack the splendor of the Five Ancients on Mount Lu;[149] the lake beside them will be dug out in a monotonous square shape, the designer mechanically placing caves below and terraces above, pavilions to the east and gazebos to the west. The cracks from poor construction will allow you to see right through, however dimly, and the paths among them will force you to play cat and

94 (facing page) "Mountain" with lace-bark pine, He Yuan.

95 (above left) Fantastic mountain, He Yuan.

96 (above right) Mountain with water and trees, He Yuan.

mouse with yourself.[150] The small mountains will look like the decorations in a goldfish bowl and the large ones like the scenery in the haunted town of Fengdu.[151] This may satisfy people of the present day, but what a contrast to the style of the ancients!

Instead, the depths of your imagination should be full of pictures, and your feelings should overflow into hills and valleys. Before the mountain heights are built up, the foothills should first come into existence, so that the structure grows more precipitous in a natural progression. Soil may be thrown up crosswise to form a ridge, so that the outline does not depend entirely on the intriguing shape of individual rocks.

Some sites may be suitable for terraces and some for gazebos, from which to entertain the moon and summon up the clouds. Paths and tracks will form themselves naturally, along which to search for flowers and explore for willows. The edges of ponds should be faced with chunks of stone, while hefty rocks can be used in appropriate places. As mountain-tops are built up from loads of soil, the variations in height form an attractive view. You cannot learn the secret of heaping up soil unless you follow the inner principles of arranging rocks. The hidden significance of mountains and forests needs deep study, whereas the temperament of flowers and trees is easy to grasp. If you have the real thing within you when you make the imitation, the imitation that you make will become real. After the inspiration of genius, completion depends on the labor of men. Those who seek the exceptional and yearn for what is fine must all come to share in this knowledge.

Mountains in Private Gardens. No-one constructs a mountain in his private garden unless he is a gentlemen and an amateur of landscape. Anyone who does this must have exceptional knowledge and appreciation. Because the world lacks people who share this interest, most people cannot appreciate the art to the full, and the best they can manage is a cliff face before their courtyard, or three peaks facing a tower. If these are arranged sparsely enough they can still achieve a good effect.

Mountains in Courtyards. People are always constructing mountains in front of their courtyards, so that three lofty peaks stick up in the midst of the surrounding walls, arranged in line before you; this looks exceptionally ridiculous. They top them with pavilions, but when you climb up there, there is absolutely no view to look at, so where is the advantage in setting them up? This is even more ridiculous. My opinion is, if you have some fine trees in your courtyard, then arrange some delicately shaped rocks around them; if not, then build up a cliff face on the inside of the walls and perhaps plant some flowering shrubs or hanging creepers above it, and thus you can achieve the effect of distance.

Mountains beside Towers. If you construct a mountain beside a tower, it ought to be as high as possible in order to be attractive. But at the same time if it is too high there is a risk of it looking too oppressive. So it is preferable to construct it rather further away from the building; this will give more of a feeling of distance.

Mountains beside Belvederes. Belvederes are open on all four sides, so they fit very well on the flank of a mountain. If the mountain is smooth and easy to climb, this is convenient for ascending the building to look at the view, and it means there is no need for a staircase.

Mountains beside Studios. Usually when smaller mountains are constructed, they will either be set around with fine trees and plants, arranged now in groups, now scattered, or be built with jutting cliffs and steep precipices, full of individuality; these are most suitable for the surroundings of studios. If you also use the rocks of the mountain to form pools, you can lean out of your windows and enjoy the feeling of being on the banks of the Hao or Pu.[152]

Mountains beside Ponds. To have mountains situated beside a pool is the finest sight in a garden. When the mountains vary in size, it is an even finer spectacle. You may set stepping-stones in the water or build a flying bridge across from the mountain side. Caves and fissures may be concealed within the mountain, running right through the cliffs or leading down to the water. The shimmering mountain tops let the moonlight through and gather the clouds. Never say there are no Immortals on earth, for this is a fairy-land in the world of men.

Mountains in the Women's Apartments. If mountains are constructed among the women's apartments, they should be firm and tall, with sheer cliffs which cannot be climbed. The reason they should be solidly built is as a precaution in case children play on them.

Precipitous Mountains. What are known as precipitous mountains are built up against walls, so that the whitewashed surface acts as paper and the rocks as the painting upon it. The designer should follow the natural cracks in the stone, imitating the brushwork of the old masters. The rocks should be planted with pines from Huangshan, ancient plum trees and fine bamboo.[153] Looking at this

scene through a round window is just like seeing scenery reflected in a mirror.

Mountain Rock Pools. I was the first person to make pools using mountain rocks. If you select thin, flat rocks to make a pool, it will not hold water if there is the least gap, so you need to be familiar with the laws of dynamic balance.[154] In arranging pieces of rock, you should weight them down firmly on three or four sides. If you only make them firm on two sides, there is a danger of damage to the stones which are laid flat on the bottom of the pond. If you only make one side firm, as soon as a slight crack appears, the water cannot be kept in, and even if you strengthen it with putty you will not be able to stop it. So you must proceed with circumspection.

Goldfish Tanks. In the same way as you can construct mountain rock pools, you can use one or two rough earthenware tanks set beside each other to make the base for a goldfish tank. You can bury the tanks completely or half bury them and build up rocks around them, filling in around the rim of the tanks with putty. If you raise fish according to the correct methods, it is best to place some miniature mountain scenery in the tank.

Sharp Peaks. If you use a single rock to form a sharp peak on a mountain, you should give consideration to its shape and choose a jagged rock suitable for a peak. Get a workman to drill a mortise and make a base for it. It should be set up so that the upper part is larger than the lower in order for it to make

99 (above) Mountain beside a "tower" (two-storey building), Ge Yuan. This is unusually close to the building.

97 (facing page top) Mountain in courtyard, He Yuan. As there is plenty of space available, there is no feeling that the mountain's size is oppressive.

98 (facing page bottom) Another courtyard mountain in the He Yuan. The delicate construction and the abundance of vegetation prevent any feeling of oppressiveness.

100 "Precipitous mountain": rocks forming cliff face against wall, Ge Yuan.

101 Entrance to cave in rock-work, Ge Yuan.

102 Looking out from inside a cave, Huanxiu Shanzhuang, Suzhou.

a fine spectacle. If you fit two or three rocks together to make the peak, they should also be larger above than below, and thus they will have the appearance of being about to soar into the air. The same applies if a number of rocks are fitted together; you should use two or three large ones to finish off the summit. You need to understand the principles of balance in order to arrange the rocks without anything going wrong. If they are just slightly tilted to one side, they will get more and more tilted as time goes on and the peak will inevitably collapse. You should take great care about this when setting them up.

Rounded Peaks. The rounded peak refers to the highest part of a mountain top and it cannot be level or the shape of a brush-rest.[155] It should be high in some parts and low in others, and it is best if it appears casually piled up in harmony with the surroundings, rather than carefully arranged.

Overhanging Cliffs. If you are constructing an overhanging cliff, you should start from a small base, making it larger as you build it up. When you reach the desired height, strengthen the back part so that you can balance the construction of the overhang. Traditionally, this method of construction is very rarely seen. Most designers can only manage to get a single rock to form the overhang and are unable to add to it. But I make use of the principles of balance, and spread the weight of the overhanging front part while making the back very firm; I also use long pieces of rock embedded in a trench to weigh down the overhanging part so than it can project for several feet. This looks most alarming, but not a single accident has ever occurred.

Caves. The method of constructing caves, as far as the base goes, is similar to that of putting up a building: you should set up a few pillars to make it firm and then put together rocks with holes in them as if to form windows and doors to let in the light. When you reach the upper part, as described previously for constructing cliffs, you should pile the stones closer together until you round off the summit, and add a longer rock to keep it all firm. In this way it will last for a thousand ages without any damage. Caves broader than ten feet or so, which can hold a number of people gathered together, have always been unusual. Above the cave you may spread earth and plant trees, or make a terrace, or construct pavilions and buildings, whichever is most appropriate.

Mountain Torrents. It is always best if artificial mountains can have water among them, but if they are on high ground and you cannot lead water up to them, then construct the bed of a mountain torrent and, even though it has no water in it, it will still have an effective presence.

Meanders.[156] In the old days meanders were all constructed by drilling out a channel in the rock and setting stone dragon-heads above it to spurt out water, but this is both wasteful of effort and vulgar in effect. Why not use the same method as in constructing a mountain torrent, with rocks above forming a spring like a waterfall? This too can provide a flow of water to carry wine cups

and has the added attraction of looking natural.

Waterfalls. Waterfalls are like "precipitous mountains" in their method of construction.[157] When forming them, first make sure you have a channel to collect the water from the eaves of the high buildings, and then direct it as a stream to the top of a wall, which will form an aqueduct and lead it to the summit of your cliff.[158] Here you must leave a small gap for the water to spurt through the rocks and cascade downwards just like a natural waterfall. Otherwise the water will just run away in all directions and not form a cascade; this will merely give an effect which can be described as "sitting in the rain and gazing at a spring."[159]

When constructing artificial mountains, you must try to achieve the very best you can, inducing others to admire them also. Although they are really just fragments of mountain and chunks of stone, they should have a feel of the wilderness about them.

Around Tiger Hill in Suzhou and Phoenix Terrace Gate in Nanjing,[160] the miniature landscapes constructed by flower-sellers all aim to achieve this.

2 Selection of Rocks

In order to learn where rocks can be obtained, you must seek far and near through the mountains. No price need be paid to the mountains for the rocks; the only expense is the labor. You must climb up and search as far as the mountain-tops, winding hither and yon to the end of the road. It is most convenient if the rocks can be transported by water, and then it does not matter if they are a thousand miles distant; however, if it does not take too long to get to them, they can be carried on shoulder poles. In picking out interesting rocks,

103 Part of what is supposed to be the original meander at the Orchid Pavilion, Shaoxing. For an imaginary version, see plate II.

do not limit yourself to elaborate ones resembling filigree; they must also be able to stand alone. In seeking out strong stones, you should also look for solid, hefty ones, which can be piled on top of each other. You should first select good quality rocks with no cracks, and then fit the jagged edges together. If there are too many cracks there is a danger of their breaking, though if they are concave they may be used to form an overhanging precipice. From ancient times, the rocks from the Great Lake have been most famous;[161] other than these, amateurs of landscape only knew the name of the "patterned rocks."[162] Nowadays people simply choose rocks from illustrations;[163] what does the ignorant multitude know of the beauty of Huangshan? Small-scale mountains should imitate the work of the Master of the Cloud Forest, and large ones should honor the style of Zijiu.[164] The individual pieces of rock may look clumsy and awkward, but when piled up they will seem all the more awe-inspiring. This sort of rock is good for arranging together, and moreover can be collected anywhere in the mountains. Rocks are not like plants or trees; once gathered, they gain a new lease of life. People, too, not content with achieving nothing, are prepared to seek fame and fortune however far this takes them.[165]

Rocks from the Great Lake. Of the rocks from the edge of the water beside Dongting Hill in Suzhou Prefecture, the best are those from Xiaoxia Bay.[166] They are naturally firm and glossy, and contain in them such shapes as "deep hollows," "eyeholes," "twists," and "strange grooves."[167] They are of various colors: white, grayish-black, and blackish-grey. The striations of the rock formation run criss-cross over them or swirl around them, rising and falling. There are pits and hollows all over the surface of the stone. These are formed by the attacks of wind and waves, and are known as "bullet holes." When tapped the rocks give out a faint sound. The workmen who gather these rocks take their mallets and drills and go into the deep water, select a rock of an interesting shape and chisel it away, then bind it with a thick rope and suspend it from a large boat; then they arrange a wooden framework and hoist the rock up out of the water. These rocks are valued for their size and height, and are particularly suitable for setting up individually before a gallery or hall, or for placing below a lofty pine-tree or strangely shaped plant. If formed into artificial mountains or set about through a park or among scattered pavilions, they make a particularly fine spectacle. They have been collected for a very long time, from ancient times until the present, so they are nowadays not easy to come by.

Rocks from Kunshan. The rocks in the ground near Ma'anshan in Kunshan

104 Lan Ying (1585–c.1666), *Deep Autumn on Mount Hua* (Shanghai Museum). Two gentlemen enjoy the sight and sound of a waterfall in the mountains.

County are covered by red soil.[168] Once they have been dug out of the ground, you have to spend an inordinate amount on having them picked free of soil and washed down. They are knobbly in shape and stretch up into the air, without the sloping shoulders of a more rounded mountain peak, and when you tap them they give out no sound. Their color is pure white. They can be set about with small trees, or have irises planted in their interstices,[169] or else they can be set in troughs to make the focal point of a miniature landscape. They cannot be put to any major use.

Rocks from Yixing. The rocks from the mountains in the area around Master Zhang's Cave and Shanjuan's Temple in Yixing County can be conveniently transported by water from their bamboo groves.[170] They are hard, with eyeholes and strange grooves like those from the Great Lake. One kind is black, coarse-grained, with some yellow in it; another kind is white and smooth-grained. If used to form mountains they cannot be made into overhanging cliffs as they may be too weak to hold firm.

Rocks from Dragon Pool. The area from Dragon Pool, about twenty-five miles downstream from Nanjing, by the banks of the Yangtze, where there is a place called Seven Stars Convent, down to Hillmouth and Granary Head, produces several types of rock, some which appear above ground and some which are half-buried.[171] One type is grey and hard, with cracks and holes going right through it, like those from the Great Lake. Another type is pale grey and hard and seems rather clumsy, but can be used to form either the foot or the summit of a mountain. Another type is mottled and rough, without holes, and suitable for standing on its own. Another type is grey, with many markings like the wrinkles of a walnut. It gives an excellent effect if these rocks can be arranged together so that the cracks look like brushwork in a painting.

Rocks from Green Dragon Hill.[172] There are rocks from Green Dragon Hill in Nanjing which have large, twisting holes in them, but these are all enhanced

106 Zhou Chen (early 16th century), *Mountain Dwelling in Summer* (Shanghai Museum). The vertical forms of the rocky peaks in the background are echoed in the "strange rock" in the right foreground, which seems to have been placed there for a decorative purpose, like a Great Lake rock, while the square forms of the rocks on the left suggest Huang rocks.

Their color is pure white, but they are mostly covered in red earth and you need to brush and wash them before you can see their natural appearance. Alternatively you can use the water running down from the guttering in the plum-rain season to wash away the color of the earth.[179] These rocks, particularly, ought to be kept for a long time, and the older they are the whiter they get so that they become just like a snowy mountain. One type is called "horsetooth xuan" and can be used as a table ornament.[180]

Rocks from Hukou. There are several types of rock from Hukou in Jiangzhou, some from under water and some from the edge of the water.[181] One type is grey in color and appears naturally in the shapes of pointed and rounded peaks, cliffs and gullies, or looking like all kinds of natural objects. Another type is flat and thin with deep hollows and eyeholes running right through the stone, very like a plank of wood planed down with a sharp blade. The striations in the stone are like the bristles in a brush, and the color is also slightly glossy. When struck they emit a sound. Su Dongpo[182] expressed his appreciation of these stones, and regarded them as "Jiuhua mountains in a pint pot"; it is to them that he refers in the line: "To buy this delicate little thing with a hundred pieces of gold."[183]

Ying Rocks. Between Hanguang and Zhenyang Counties in Yingzhou, there are several types of rocks, which are found in stream beds.[184] One type is light grey with white veins winding through it. Another type is slightly grayish black, and another is a pale green, and they all have the shapes of pointed or rounded peaks with concavities and eyeholes that twist around and interconnect. The texture of this rock is slightly glossy, and a faint sound echoes when it is struck. These rocks can be set out as table ornaments or used as a feature of interest with a potted plant, or put together to form a miniature landscape. There is another type which is white in color, with peaks which thrust up on all sides into many projecting points. It is slightly translucent, with reflective surfaces in which objects can be mirrored. When struck it does not resonate. The workmen who gather these rocks go into the water and select attractive pieces to chisel out. They can be used only as table ornaments.

Rocks from San Bing. San Bing, meaning Routed Soldiers, is the place where Zhang Liang of the Han dynasty made his own soldiers sing the songs of Chu and thus upset and routed the Chu army, hence the name.[185] It is situated to the south of Lake Chao (Chao Hu), and has rocks of all sizes and every possible shape poking up all over the hills.[186] The stone is firm and blue-black in color. Some rocks are like those of the Great Lake, some are awkwardly shaped and covered with jagged edges. The local people collect them and carry them out to sell, and amateurs of landscape in Yangzhou buy nothing but this kind of rock.[187] The finest of them are large, intriguing, and perforated like Great Lake Rocks. None finer than these have yet been collected.

Huang Rocks. Huang rocks are obtainable all over the place.[188] Their texture is firm and does not admit the adze or chisel, and the striations in the stone are rough and coarse. Places such as Huangshan near Changzhou, Yaofengshan near Suzhou, Tushan near Zhenjiang, and all along the Yangtze to above Caishi all produce these rocks.[189] Vulgar people are aware only of their hefty appearance and not of their subtle attraction.

Ancient Rocks. Many amateurs of landscape in this world are over-impressed by empty fame and go to great lengths to seek out ancient rocks. They hear of such and such a peak stone from such and such a famous garden on which such and such a famous person wrote an ode which has been handed down from such and such a dynasty to the present day, and moreover that this is a genuine Great Lake rock, but now that the garden has gone to ruin the present owners are selling the rocks to the highest bidder; they don't begrudge any amount of money to buy it, actually regarding it as a valuable antique. Other people only have to hear that a rock is ancient to buy it for an enormous price. From the past to the present day, so many Great Lake rocks have been removed by collectors that it seems there are not many left. If you can find and collect rocks with perforations or "grey bones,"[190] hard in texture, from other mountains which have not yet been exploited, they will not necessarily be inferior to those of the Great Lake. When a rock has been exposed to the winds for countless ages, what do expressions like "new" and "old" really mean? If you collect rocks, even though you only need to pay the expenses of shipment and labor for loading and unloading, think how much you actually have to spend to get a rock into your garden. I heard of a rock known as "Hundred Rice Peak," and on enquiry I learnt that the name arose because it cost a hundred bushels of rice to acquire.[191] Nowadays you would have to pay a hundred bushels of rice to buy it and another hundred for transport, so it would have to be called "Two Hundred Rice Peak." Any rock which has been exposed to the winds is ancient, and any which has just been dug out of the earth is new, but even if it is discolored with earth it only has to stand out in the rain and dew for a while and it too will become "ancient."

Jinchuan Rocks.[192] These rocks are preferable if ancient. There are five-colored ones, and pure green ones, and ones with markings like pine-tree bark in a painting. The most valuable are more than ten feet tall and a full foot across, but the majority are shorter. Recently rocks like those from Jinchuan have been coming from Yixing, but they have pebbles embedded in the cracks and eyeholes, nor is the color so good. The cracks and eyeholes of the ancient ones are quite empty and their color and texture are clear and glossy. They look very elegant when set upright among flowers or under trees. If used to form artificial mountains, they are particularly appropriate as "split peaks."

The Patterned Rock Convoy. The patterned rocks from the Song dynasty appear all over the area of Henan which borders on Shandong.[193] These were the rocks left behind during transportation. Many of these rocks are extremely intriguing. Because the route overland is very difficult, collectors take just a

few pieces to place in their gardens, but even so they add considerable interest.

Pebbles from Luhe. Among the sand and by the edge of the water at Spiritual Dwelling Cliff in Luhe County are found agate pebbles which are very fine and small.[194] Some are as large as a fist, pure white with five-colored marking. Others have the five-colored markings only. They are very warm-looking, glossy and translucent. If you pick out the ones with fine colors and patterns you can use them to lay a floor like brocade. Or if you place them in the bed of a stream or anywhere with flowing water, they will appear naturally bright and shining.

As regards the construction of artificial mountains in gardens, it seems there may be amateurs of landscape everywhere, and fine pieces of rock everywhere too, but they can never find the right person to undertake the design work. If you wonder where to obtain rocks, there are mountains everywhere and they all seem to have rocks. Even if you cannot find any really attractive rocks and have to make do with rather clumsy-looking ones, they are all right as long as they have some markings on them. I have read the *Catalogue of Rocks* by Du Wan of the Song dynasty, which shows there is nowhere that rocks cannot be found.[195] The places from which I have used rocks are not many, and I have noted them briefly above. Other rocks which I have not seen I have not recorded.

3 Making Use of Natural Scenery

There are no fixed rules for designing gardens but there are certain principles in making use of the natural scenery. The essential thing is to keep in mind all the four seasons; at which point of the compass any feature is placed is of little importance. Woods and marshes are suitable for lingering in, since in them are bamboo groves and whispering forests. The clamor of cities should be avoided, so you must choose an area with few local residents. From a high plateau you can gaze to the horizon, and the distant peaks surround you like a screen. Your hall sends forth a gentle breeze to welcome the visitor, and your gate brings in a springtime stream to feed the marsh. Amid lovely red and purple blossoms you

will be happy to meet the Angel of the Flowers.[196] Enjoy the Saint and savor the Sage, and you can compare yourself to the Prime Minister in the Mountains.[197]

Spring will embody the poem on "Living as a Hermit" by Pan Yue, or Qu Yuan's affection for the fragrant herbs.[198] When sweeping your paths take care of the orchid shoots, and they will send their fragrance into your retreat. Roll up your blinds and greet the swallows who slice through the light breeze like shears. Everywhere float drifting petals and the drowsy threads of willows. If the cold still makes you shiver, hang up a high swing.[199] You can enjoy yourself at leisure and delight in the hills and valleys. Your thoughts will travel beyond the confines of this world of dust, and you will feel as though you were wandering within a painting.

From the summer shade of the woods the song of the oriole starts; in the folds of the hills you suddenly hear a wood-cutter singing and, as a breeze springs up from the cool of the forest, you feel as though you were transported

109 Summer: "Ripples cover the surface of the water." Pond where Geese Play, Yi Yuan, Nanxiang.

110 Autumn: "Rank upon rank of crimson maples flushed with wine." Pagoda of the Six Harmonies, Hangzhou.

111 Winter: "The gentleman of high ideals lies in his snow-covered cottage." Rooftops under snow, Zhenjiang.

back to the realm of the Emperor Fuxi.[200] The hermit recites poetry in his pine-wood hut, and the gentleman of leisure plucks his lute in a grove of bamboo. The red garments of the lotuses are newly washed, and the green jade of the bamboos gently chimes. You can gaze at the bamboo by a bend in the stream, and watch the fish from the banks of the Hao. Mist drifts through the mountains, and the floating clouds sink down as you lean on the railing. Ripples cover the surface of the water, and you feel a cool breeze as you recline on your pillow. On the southern verandah you express your exalted emotions,[201] and by the northern shutters you enjoy the mid-day shade.[202] Beyond the half-open window lies the emerald shade of plantains and paulownias, and vines and creepers spread their turquoise over the surrounding wall: lean over the stream and enjoy the moon; sit on a rock and savor the spring-water.

Your light summer clothes can no longer withstand the fresh chill of autumn, but the scent of the lotuses in the pond still draws you to them. The phoenix-tree leaves are startled into their autumn fall,[203] and the insects cry, hidden in the grasses. The level surface of the lake is a boundless expanse of floating light; the outline of the hills is of delicious beauty. There comes into view a skein of white egrets, and rank upon rank of crimson maples flushed with wine. You gaze afar from a high terrace, rub your eyes and wonder at the clear sky; leaning over the void from a spacious pavilion, you raise your glass and hail the bright moon.[204] Imperceptibly a heavenly fragrance steals around as the osmanthus seeds sadly fall.[205]

You notice that beside the withered hedge the chrysanthemum flowers are over; it is winter now, time to explore the warmer hillsides to see if the first plum blossoms are out. You should tie a little money to your staff and invite your rustic neighbors to a drink.[206] The plum flower is like a lovely woman coming from the moonlit woods, while the gentleman of high ideals lies in his snow-covered cottage.[207] The lowering clouds are wintry grey; the few leaves left on the trees rustle together. Wind-blown crows perch on some sparse trees in the setting sun; cold-driven geese utter a few cries under the waning moon. Waking from a dream by the window of his study, a solitary figure recites poetry to himself. The brocade curtain huddles round the glowing brazier; the six-petaled flowers of snowflakes offer their benison. You can set out in a boat as if passing the stream of Yan,[208] or sweep up snow and boil it, making tea better than the wine of the Dang clan.[209] Elegant activities can still be carried on in the winter's cold, and you can equal famous men of refinement in the past. There are few flowers that do not wither, but fresh scenes can be enjoyed all year round.

There is no definite way of making the most of scenery; you know it is right when it stirs your emotions.

Making use of the natural scenery is the most vital part of garden design. There are various aspects such as using scenery in the distance, near at hand, above you, below you, and at certain times of the year. But the attraction of natural objects, both the form perceptible to the eye and the essence which touches the heart, must be fully imagined in your mind before you put pen to paper, and only then do you have a possibility of expressing it completely.

AFTERWORD

In the Jiaxu year of the Chongzhen era [1634] I was fifty-three years old. I had been through many stormy experiences, and was already tired of my wanderings in the course of my profession. In my youth I had a deep interest in woodlands, and evaded fame among the hills and valleys. For a long time I made a living from landscape gardening. I felt as though I was cut off from the things of this world, and only heard distantly of the turmoil of current events.[210] I had a deep desire to become a hermit but unfortunately I did not have the power to purchase a mountain of my own.[211] I would gladly have lived by the outflow of the Peach Blossom Spring![212] I sighed to myself that I was born at the wrong time. Zhuge Liang, Marquis of Wu, was a counselor of the Three Kingdoms; Di Renjie, Duke of Liang, was Prime Minister to Empress Wu Zetian—and these ancient heroes were also prevented from achieving all they might have done by the times they lived in.[213] How much the more so for me, a coarse and foolish fellow from the wild countryside, spending my days among hills and valleys. In my free time I compiled this manual, intending it for the instruction of my two sons, Changsheng and Changji, but they, like Tao Yuanming's son, are only capable of hunting for pears and chestnuts.[214] So I have had it printed and published for the benefit of society.

112 Liu Songnian (fl. 1190-1224), *Reading at the Window in Autumn* (Liaoning Provincial Museum).

Appendix

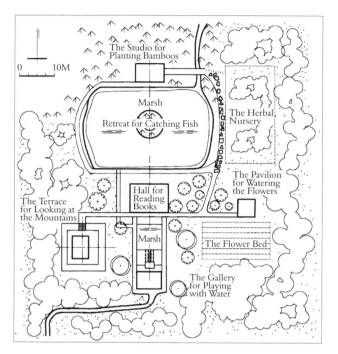

The Studio for
Planting Bamboos

0   10M

Marsh
Retreat for Catching Fish

The Herbal
Nursery

The Pavilion
for Watering
the Flowers

The Terrace
for Looking at
the Mountains

Hall for
Reading
Books

Marsh

The Flower Bed

The Gallery
for Playing
with Water

113 Sima Guang's Garden of Solitary
Delight: a modern reconstruction of the
layout by Professor Wang Duo, based on
Sima Guang's description.

Sima Guang: *The Garden of Solitary Delight*[215]

Mencius said: "To delight in pleasure by oneself is not as good as taking pleasure together with the multitude; and to take pleasure with the few is not as good as taking pleasure together with the multitude." This is the pleasure of princes and nobles and cannot be attained by the poor and lowly. Confucius said: "To eat rice and vegetables and drink water, and then pillow one's head on one's arm: it is here that pleasure lies;" and Master Yan: "A bowlful to eat and a ladleful to drink: this is a pleasure that need not be forgone."[216] This is the pleasure of saints and sages and cannot be attained by the ignorant. Now when the tailor-bird nests in the wood, it occupies no more than one branch, and when the tapir drinks from the river, it takes no more than will fill its belly; each takes its allotted portion and is content, and this is what I, the Old Pedant, delight in also.[217]

In the fourth year of the Xining period [1071] I first made my home in Luoyang,[218] and in the sixth year [1073] I bought twenty *mu* of land by the north gate of the Zunxian District to make a garden. I built a hall in the middle, in which I placed five thousand volumes from my library, and named it "Hall for Reading Books." South of the hall was a group of rooms, and I directed a watercourse to flow northwards and pass below the buildings. In the center I made a marsh, three feet wide and deep, and I separated the water into five streams running into the marsh in the form of a tiger's claws. From the north side of the marsh the water flowed underground and came out by the north steps, from where it cascaded into the courtyard like an elephant's trunk. From here it was divided into two channels and flowed round the four corners of the courtyard, meeting again in the north-west corner, from where it flowed away. This area was named "The Gallery for Playing with Water."

North of the hall was a marsh with an island in the middle, and on the island I planted bamboo in a ring like a jade circlet, thirty feet around, and I bound the tops together like a fisherman's hut, and called it "Retreat for Catching Fish." North of the marsh was a building lying crosswise, with six columns and with extremely thick walls to ward off the heat of the sun. You could open a door to get out to the east, while along the north and south sides were set large windows to catch the cool breezes. In front of and behind it were planted many beautiful bamboos to make a cool place in the summer heat, and it was named "The Studio for Planting Bamboos." To the east of the marsh I divided the ground into one hundred and twenty plots and planted all sorts of herbs, labeling them with their names. To the north of this plot I planted bamboo in a square pattern like a chess-board, ten feet across; I bent over the tops of the bamboos and joined them together to make a house. I also planted bamboo in front of this, enclosing a path like a portico, and covered it all with climbing herbs, and on all four sides I planted medicinal trees, making a fence; I named it "The Herbal Nursery." To the south of the nursery I placed six railings, two each supporting peonies, tree-peonies, and mixed flowers; I only planted two plants of each type, just enough to become familiar with their appearance and no more.[219] To the north of these railings was a pavilion which I named "The Pavilion for Watering the Flowers." The city of Luoyang is not far from the mountains, but owing to the dense and flourishing growth of the woods, it is seldom possible to see the mountains; therefore I constructed a terrace in the middle of the garden, and put up a building on top of it in order to get a view of Wan'an, Xuanyuan and even as far as Taishi mountains, and I named this "The Terrace for Looking at the Mountains."

I spent most of my time in the study reading my books. I found teachers among the wise men superior to me, and friends among the mass of worthy folk.[220] We speculated on the origins of benevolence and virtue, and explored the laws of ritual and music. From before the beginning of creation, and stretching beyond the limits of the four directions—the principles of all things corporeal and incorporeal were all present to our gaze. My weakness was that my learning was inadequate, but on the other hand I asked nothing of anyone and needed nothing from the external world. When mind and body were both weary, I could cast my rod and catch fish, or gather herbs in my skirt, or open the channels to irrigate my plants, or wield an axe to chop down bamboo, then bathe my hands in warm water, and climb to a high place and gaze as far as my eyes could see, wandering freely exactly as I wished. The bright moon would appear at the appointed time, the fresh breeze would arrive of its own volition. There was nothing to drag me along and nothing to impede me; my ears, eyes, lungs and guts were all under my own control, alone and uninhibited. I don't know what other pleasure there is between heaven and earth that can take the place of this. So I named the whole place "The Garden of Solitary Delight." Some people criticized me, saying: "I have heard it said that the gentleman must share his pleasure with others, but now you find satisfaction in solitude, and do not extend your pleasure to others; this is unacceptable."[221] I excused myself, saying: "I am just an old fool; how can I be compared with a gentleman? I am afraid the pleasure I get on my own is not sufficient; how could I extend it to others? Moreover, what I take pleasure in is poor, mean, low and uncivilized, in fact everything that the world rejects; even if I were to shove it at people, they would still not accept it, so how could I force it on them? If there were anyone willing to share this pleasure, I would bow down and present it to him; I would never dare to keep it to myself!"

Notes

1   The Jianwen Emperor (503–551) of the Liang dynasty reigned for only two years, 550–551. He is said to have remarked of the park or garden known as the Flowery Forest: "A place that fulfills one's heart's desire does not need to be remote. Behind a screen of trees, one's thoughts can be at ease as on the banks of Hao or Pu, and one feels that all the birds, beasts and fishes are one's closest friends."

2   See note 44.

3   Chen Zhongzi was from the kingdom of Qi (present-day Shandong province) in the Warring States period (fifth to third centuries BC). He was famous for enduring poverty for the sake of his principles, but Mencius was of the opinion that "pushed to the utmost limits, his way of life would only be possible if he were an earthworm." (III.B.10. References to Mencius are to D.C. Lau's translation, published by Penguin Classics.)

4   See note 156. I have elsewhere used "meander" as a generic term for the type of winding stream found at the Orchid Pavilion, which I have here called the Serpentine.

5   Wangchuan was the country estate in Lantian County, Shaanxi, of Wang Wei (701?–761), the great Buddhist poet and painter of the Tang dynasty. The Deer Enclosure and Dappled Apricots were names of particular features of the Wangchuan estate. Wang Wei wrote a series of short poems describing different scenes on the estate. The Deer Enclosure was the subject of one of the most famous of them:

> In the empty mountains no-one is to be seen;
> I only hear the sound of human voices.
> The sun casts slanting shadows into the depths of the wood
> And shines down on the green moss.

The later poet Su Dongpo praised Wang Wei with the words: "In his poems there are paintings, and in his paintings there is poetry."

6   The Bogeywoman (Mo Mu, or Mother Mo), a legendary ugly woman, was supposedly the fourth concubine of the Yellow Emperor.

7   In Chinese, it is actually the pigeon which is too clumsy to build its own nest and has to occupy that of the magpie.

8   The *Rites of Zhou* (*Zhou Li*): one of the ancient Confucian classics, recording the court rituals of the Zhou dynasty (eleventh to third centuries BC). The "Record of All Crafts" was not originally part of it, but was added in the Han dynasty to replace a chapter lost when the First Emperor of the Qin dynasty (221–206 BC) "burnt the books and buried the scholars" in an attempt to wipe out Confucianism.

9   Zheng Yuanxun (1603–1644) was originally from Anhui but transferred his registered place of residence to Yizheng County, Jiangsu, near the city of Yangzhou. He was a poet and painter, and in 1632 started to create the Garden of Shade from an abandoned site to the south of the county town of Jiangdu. The name "Garden of Shade" was thought up and inscribed by the great painter Dong Qichang, then living at Yangzhou. In 1634 Ji Cheng became involved in the design of the garden. Zheng Yuanxun graduated as a *jinshi* (advanced scholar) in 1643, but was killed the next year, at the early age of 42, by Ming loyalists defending Yangzhou who mistakenly thought that he had come to an agreement with the enemy.

10   Two wandering hermits of the Eastern Han dynasty (25–220); history records little more than their names.

11   The first chapter of the Daoist classic *Zhuang Zi* is entitled "Free and Easy Wandering."

12   The Luan River is the river of Yizheng County in Jiangsu. The county itself is sometimes known as Luanjiang or Luan River. For the Wu Garden, see notes 27 and 97.

13   Songling or Pine Ridge is present-day Wujiang in Jiangsu. This was where Ji Cheng's family came from; their home was in a town called Tongli.

14   For Cao Yuanfu and his role in the naming of *The Craft of Gardens*, see Ji Cheng's own preface with note 28.

15   The coat of many colors (literally "five-colored garment") refers to a preposterous but well-known story of a man distinguished for filial piety who, at the age of seventy, would dress up in the colorful garments appropriate to a child and gambol about to make his even more aged parents feel that they were young again.

16   Ruan Dacheng (1587–1646) was a prominent late Ming official. Stone Nest was his estate in his native Anqing, in present-day Anhui province. After the downfall in 1627 of the eunuch Wei Zhongxian, with

whom he was associated, Ruan also lost his job and went to live in retirement in Nanjing. His mansion was in a street called Kusifang or Granary Office Lane, known to the irreverent as Kuzidang or Trouser Crotch. It was at this time that he assembled a large household of wandering swordsmen and other persons with special skills such as Ji Cheng himself; Ruan also owned a private publishing concern, which printed and published Ji Cheng's book. Ruan Dacheng was later rehabilitated and appointed Minister of Defense, but then surrendered to the invading Manchus and died not long afterwards.

17 Guan Tong was a painter of the Later Liang dynasty (907–923), famous for his landscapes showing forests in autumn. A pupil of Jing Hao, he reputedly surpassed his master, and established a forceful style of painting which was one of the main currents in Five Dynasties and Northern Song painting.

Jing Hao was a scholar of the Later Liang who lived as a hermit in the Taihang mountains and wrote on art theory as well as painting landscapes in the Tang style.

18 The ancient kingdom of Chu, which flourished in the fourth and third centuries BC, covered approximately the region of present-day Hunan and Hubei in central China.

19 The region of Wu—which was the name of one of the kingdoms of which ancient China was composed—is equivalent to present-day Jiangsu province. Zhenjiang, a city on the Yangtze River, was known in Ji Cheng's day as Runzhou, and this is how he refers to it here.

20 Gou Mang, the God of Spring, was also known as the Tree God or the Green Emperor. The custom to which Ji Cheng refers appears in fact to have died out in early times and to be known to him only from literary sources. This may therefore be one of Ji Cheng's characteristic rather unnecessary displays of learning.

21 Ji Cheng refers to Changzhou under its ancient name of Jinling (not the same as the Jinling which is the old name for Nanjing). Wu Youyu, whose personal name was Xuan, was from the Changzhou area and graduated as a *jinshi* (advanced scholar) in the reign of the Wanli emperor (1573–1620). He called himself "The Daoist of Shuai" and published a book of essays under this name.

22 The *mu* is the traditional Chinese measurement of area; it is still used despite the adoption of the metric system. 15 *mu* is about 2.47 acres.

23 The Khan of Wen had been an officer in the Mongol army; the Yuan (Mongol) dynasty lasted from 1279 to 1368.

24 Sima Guang lived from 1019 to 1086 and was a minister of the Song court. He wrote the great historical work *Comprehensive Mirror to Aid in Government* (*Zi Zhi Tong Jian*). It is not clear whether it is a coincidence that his posthumously granted fiefdom of Wen was the same as that of the former owner of Wu Youyu's garden, or whether it was this that suggested to Wu the idea of copying the Garden of Solitary Delight. Sima Guang wrote a famous description of this garden, which he had constructed in his retirement at Luoyang, in Henan, while he was out of favor at court (see Appendix).

25 South of the River (Jiangnan): the Yangtze is the River *par excellence*, and the phrase "South of the River" is used to refer to the cultural heartland of China, particularly the area of present-day Jiangsu and Zhejiang provinces.

26 Wang Shiheng, whose identity is unclear, was a friend of Ruan Dacheng, whose collected works include four poems addressed to Wang.

27 Luan River (Luanjiang) is the present Yizheng County in Jiangsu. The garden designed for Secretary Wang was evidently the Wu Garden seen and enjoyed by Ruan Dacheng (see his introduction, On the "Craft"). Ji Cheng also refers in his section on Covered Walkways to the Seal Cloud Walkway which he designed for the Wu Garden.

28 Cao Yuanfu, whose personal name was Lüji, graduated as a *jinshi* in 1616. He was a prolific writer and a friend of Ji Cheng's patron Ruan Dacheng. Gushu is present-day Dangtu in Anhui.

29 No doubt Ji Cheng was delighted to have his work compared to these masters (see note 17).

30 Lu Ban, the patron saint or ancestor of carpenters, is here referred to by an alternative surname, Gongshu. Lu Ban seems to have been entirely legendary, whereas Lu Yun apparently lived in the Jin dynasty (third century) and wrote on the craft of foundation-laying.

31 "A mere mechanic": literally "a person without orifices," i.e. someone lacking in human sensitivities.

32 The word *jian* (room-space or span) refers to the lateral space between the pillars of a building. Thus a building with six pillars in the façade will have five *jian*. Each *jian* may or may not form a separate room. Given the limitations of a single piece of timber, a *jian* can be thought of as a more or less standard measure of space. The depth (*jin*) is the space from front to back.

33 The word translated throughout as gazebo is *xie*. No clear distinction is drawn by Ji Cheng between a gazebo and a pavilion (*ting*). Both are small, open structures intending for resting in the shade (or out of the rain) and admiring the view.

34 See note 30.

35 The Chinese "orchid" (*lanhua*) is actually *cymbidium virens*, not a true orchid. The Chinese term is in fact

fairly vague, and different types of *lan* cover a variety of monocotyledonous plants.

Angelica (*zhi*) is *angelica anomala*.

36 The "three auspicious things" may be pine, bamboo and plum (*prunus mume*—actually a type of apricot), also known as the "three friends in winter," or they may be prunus, bamboo and rocks.

37 "Many acres": literally "a thousand *qing*" (one *qing* = approximately sixteen acres), which poetically balances the "four seasons." These parallelisms, an essential part of Chinese poetry and prose, usually come over very awkwardly in English (and sometimes in Chinese too). Ji Cheng uses them constantly but it is often impossible to retain them in translation.

38 Phoenix tree: *firmiana simplex* or *sterculia platanifolia*, also known as the parasol tree. But Ji Cheng may also be thinking of the paulownia tree (*paulownia fortunei*). Pagoda tree: *sophora japonica* (Japanese pagoda, Chinese scholar tree).

39 Li Zhaodao, a painter of the Tang dynasty. He followed his father Li Sixun (651–716) as a landscape painter. One of his reputed works, *A Journey through the Mountains in Spring,* survives, as does one of his father's.

40 This refers to one of the many types of brush-stroke which had to be mastered by the student of landscape painting.

41 Dachi or, to give his full title, Dachi Daoren (the Daoist of Great Folly) was the Yuan dynasty painter Huang Gongwang or Huang Zijiu (1269–1354). He was chiefly a landscape painter, from Changshu in Jiangsu, famous for his jagged rocks and grand landscapes. Ji Cheng often refers to his work. At one time Huang was imprisoned for allegedly embezzling taxes and, on his release, worked as a geomancer around the Hangzhou area. He was a poet, composer and calligrapher as well as a painter.

42 The cry of cranes is a Daoist equivalent to Buddhism's Sanskrit chants. Cranes were regarded as a symbol of long life—perhaps because of their regular return from migration—and thus were associated with Daoist immortals. The red patch on the head of the red-crowned crane (*grus japonensis*) is associated with the red mineral cinnabar, which was a vital ingredient in the elixirs of life concocted by the Daoists. Purple-colored mist is also associated with the appearance of Daoist sages.

43 Duckweed: *spiradela polyhiza*.

Polygonum: either *polygonum hydropiper* or *polygonum orientale*.

44 For Wang Wei (here referred to by his scholarly name, Mojie) and the Wangchuan estate, see note 5.

Shi Chong or Shi Jilun, a wealthy man of the Jin dynasty (third century), constructed and wrote about the Golden Valley Garden at Luoyang. This was one of the most famous gardens of ancient China, partly because of Shi Chong's fabulous wealth, although in his own description of the garden it appears as a simple country retreat.

45 Xiaoxia Bay, on the Great Lake (Tai Hu) near Suzhou, was once the summer residence of King Fuchai of Wu, who reigned in the early fifth century BC. Xiaoxia means "dispelling the summer (heat)" and is matched by Cangchun ("collecting spring") in a characteristic parallelism.

46 Plantain: *musa basjoo* (Japanese banana). Mermaids' tears solidify into pearls.

47 Xiaoman, referred to here as Mannü (Barbarian Girl), was a courtesan favored by the Tang poet Bai Juyi (772–846). She was a famous dancer and singer, and one of her best-known songs was *The Willow Branches*. Comparing willow trees to Xiaoman's waist became a commonplace of later poetry.

48 The seats are of course not chairs but mats on the floor. The "world of dust" is a Buddhist term. The phrase "red dust" is also used. These have become accepted metaphors for the vanity of this world.

49 One of Ji Cheng's characteristic shifts in tone from the loftily poetical to the mundanely practical. Professor Chen Congzhou is inclined to believe that Ji Cheng, being an uneducated man, employed someone else to write the poetic parts for him, with the aim of making his work acceptable to the educated class. Inadequate editing of the final text would then account for the sharp contrast in styles.

50 The jade object known as a "*bi*" is a circle with a hole in the middle. The word afterwards came to mean jade in general. In fact Ji Cheng here does not really seem to be envisaging a circular shape.

51 The expression "*bu zhu*" can simply mean to choose a location to build, but the word *bu* implies the use of geomancy, and in fact it would traditionally be most unlikely to embark on a major construction project without the assistance of a geomancer; this is the case even in present-day Hong Kong and is certainly still the case in the countryside of mainland China.

52 Ji Cheng uses the expression "*jie tian*"—to borrow from heaven—to describe the building of an overhanging construction. There was an expression used in living memory in China: "It's better to borrow from heaven than to borrow (from) the ground" (*jie tian bu jie di*); this refers to the fact that rent was only paid on housing space directly attached to the ground, so if your house or flat had a balcony built out from an upper storey, you got the extra space for nothing.

53 Again, cranes are associated with the life of the Daoist recluse (see note 42).

54 This is the first overt reference to the great poet Tao Qian or Tao Yuanming (365 or 372 or 376–427). Ji

Cheng has earlier used phrases which recall his poetry and frequently refers to or quotes him throughout this work. Tao gave up his official career (which had given him the title of Warden Tao by which he is sometimes known) in disgust at the compromises it required, and retired to live a pastoral life as a recluse. He is recorded as traveling in a litter. Tao took a generally Daoist attitude towards life, but was resigned to death rather than seeking immortality.

Xie Lingyun (385–433) had a more distinguished official career than Tao, but retired on the pretext of illness. He was an inveterate traveler and mountaineer, and he invented the special wooden climbing-clogs referred to here which could be adjusted for going up or down hill. He was one of the first great landscape poets—a romantic where Tao was pastoral—and, as an ardent Buddhist, used landscape as a metaphor for the teachings of Buddhist philosophy.

55 Peony (*shaoyao*): *paeonia albiflora*. To be distinguished from the tree-peony (*mudan*), *paeonia moutan*. Rose (*qiangwei*): *rosa centifolia*.

56 The poet Wang Kangju wrote that "the small recluse finds his retreat among hills and marshes; the great recluse finds his in the city market-place."

No doubt Ji Cheng is also thinking of one of Tao Yuanming's best-known poems:

> I built my house near where others dwell,
> And yet there is no clamor of carriages and horses.
> You ask of me "How can this be so?"
> "When the heart is far the place of itself is distant."
> I pluck chrysanthemums under the eastern hedge,
> And gaze afar towards the southern mountains.
> The mountain air is fine at evening of the day
> And flying birds return together homewards.
> Within these things there is a hint of Truth,
> But when I start to tell it, I cannot find the words.
> (Translation by William Acker)

57 This is another reference to Tao Yuanming (notes 54, 56).

58 Confucius considered himself inferior to an old peasant or gardener, presumably because he was not content with his lot.

59 The *Record of Xiangyang* related that "Xi Yu, a court official of the Han dynasty, constructed a fishpond in accordance with the instructions in 'Fan Li's Method of Raising Fish' to the south of Mount Xian. There was a high embankment along the edge of the pond, where he planted bamboo, catalpa [*catalpa bungei* or *catalpa ovata*] and hibiscus. From the green banks, water-caltrop [*trapa natans*] and *trapa bispinosa* covered the water, and it was a famous place for swallows."

60 In rainy weather the dove stays with its mate; in clear weather it calls for its mate and this call brings the rain.

61 To show their appreciation of beautiful scenery, or to commemorate an enjoyable gathering, visitors would often take a brush and write impromptu poems or comments on their host's walls. If well-written, these would be considered a valuable addition to the environment. Ji Cheng is indicating that well-written comments should be preserved, but crude or badly written remarks should be quickly whitewashed over.

62 Lord Wen is Sima Guang's title (see note 24). Sima Guang in fact describes his garden as having an area of twenty *mu*.

63 The name Little Jade is commonly used for pageboys in Tang poetry.

64 The women of a household would not normally appear when there were guests present.

65 Shi Chong (Shi Jilun) in his *Introduction to Poems of the Golden Valley* (see note 44) refers to imposing a forfeit of drinking three ladles full of wine on guests who were unable to produce a poem. See also note 156 for a famous poetry and wine contest.

66 Xie Tiao (464–499) was known as a writer on landscape and a calligrapher; he was admired as an example of culture and elegant living. His work was often compared with that of Xie Lingyun (see note 54).

67 Sun Deng was a recluse in the third century. Ruan Ji, a famous writer and one of the Seven Sages of the Bamboo Grove, frequently called on him but he never did anything but laugh loudly in response. Once when Ruan Ji had left and got half way down the hill from Sun's retreat, he heard Sun whistling "like the cry of a phoenix."

68 The Tang poet Meng Haoran (689–740) was famous for riding a donkey to go and look for plum blossoms. He wrote quiet pastoral poetry somewhat like that of Wang Wei, who was a close friend and painted his portrait.

69 In the Song dynasty, Tao Yi bought a concubine from the household of a high official surnamed Dang. When snow fell he collected it to boil and make tea, and remarked to his new concubine, "I don't suppose

the Dang family knows about this." She replied, "They are coarse people; they just fling their money around and consume lamb and fine wines." Snow-water was valued for making tea because of its purity. The art of tea drinking was perfected early on in China and the "tea ceremony" developed there before spreading to Japan.

70 The Dark is heaven and the Yellow is earth. This terminology comes from the *Book of Changes* (*Yi Jing*).

71 This refers to a story in the *History of the Jin Dynasty* about Ruan Ji (see note 67) who made a habit of literally looking down his nose at people of whom he disapproved, but straight at people whom he liked.

72 The Peak of Gou is Gou Shi Shan or the Mountain of the Gou Family, to the south of Yanshi County in Henan. An early work of history relates that in the Zhou dynasty (first millennium BC) Wang Zijin, who was an excellent flute-player, rode on a white crane, halted at the Peak of Gou on the seventh day of the seventh month, then raised his hand to bid farewell to the world and disappeared.

73 It was at the Jasper Lake that the legendary King Mu of Zhou entertained the goddess known as the Queen Mother of the West during his travels. There is a lake in the Celestial Mountains (Tian Shan) of Xinjiang which has been named after it.

74 There are many literary variations on the theme that the Daoist adept's attempts to turn into an Immortal are a waste of time and that what is truly magical or saintly is to be able to enjoy life as it comes.

75 For obvious practical reasons of maximizing warmth and light, the main building in a traditional Chinese courtyard house is always the "north room" or the building on the north side of the courtyard, which naturally faces south. The emperor in formal audience always sat facing the south. The axis of the imperial palace runs north-south and Chinese houses are almost always oriented in this way. It is characteristic of Ji Cheng's practical approach that he should regard keeping to the usual way of doing things as being much less important than ensuring an attractive view from the building (compare his warnings against paying too rigid attention to the geomancer).

76 Warden Tao is the poet Tao Yuanming (note 54). Many of his poems refer to the growing of chrysanthemums, which were his favourite flower. The flowers are associated with long life because they bloom much later than most other flowers. Consequently white chrysanthemums are much used at Chinese funerals. Chrysanthemum petals are believed to have a medicinal value and are often added to tea. An infusion of chrysanthemum flowers would be drunk at the time of the Double Ninth Festival—the ninth day of the ninth month in the Chinese calendar. The Chinese words for "nine" and "long-lasting" (*jiu*) sound the same, so there is again an association with long life.

77 Yu Sheng, sent by Emperor Wu of the Han dynasty (reigned 140–87 BC) to attack the people of Southern Yue, captured the "Southern Peak" which was thereafter known as "Yu's Peak." This hill was subsequently planted with plum trees by the distinguished Tang dynasty scholar-official and poet, Zhang Jiuling (678–740).

78 The word translated as "the path to wisdom" is actually "the ford." This refers to a story in *The Analects* about Confucius asking directions from a peasant ploughing in the fields. "Asking about the ford" became synonymous with searching for wisdom.

79 These lines come from a poem by Wang Wei (note 5), "Gazing from a height over the River Han":

> On the borders of Chu the three Xiang rivers meet;
> Through Jingmen's hills the nine tributaries reach.
> The River flows beyond the edge of the world;
> The prospect of the mountains lies between being and non-being.
> The prefectural city floats on the near river-bank,
> While its waves shake the sky in the distance.
> Amid these fine views of Xiangyang,
> I linger, drunken, with Old Master Shan.

("Old Master Shan" was Shan Jian, one of the Seven Sages of the Bamboo Grove in the third century. He was at one time a military governor in Xiangyang but was chiefly renowned for his drinking. Wang Wei means that only Shan Jian—who had lived some five hundred years previously—would be capable of fully appreciating the landscape here.)

80 See note 32.

81 What Ji Cheng means by this is a mystery to me.

82 This is a quotation from a well-known poem, "On Climbing Stork Tower" by Wang Zhihuan (688–742), an otherwise rather obscure poet:

> The bright sun disappears beyond the mountains;
> The Yellow River flows towards the sea.
> If you want to see a thousand miles into the distance,
> Then climb up one more storey.

83 The reference is to a story from the *Zhuang Zi*:

> Master Zhuang and Master Hui were going for a walk by the bridge over the River Hao. Master Zhuang remarked: "Look how the fish dart about so carefree. This is how fish enjoy themselves." Master Hui said: "You are not a fish; how do you know what fish enjoy?" Master Zhuang replied: "You are not me; how do you know I don't know what fish enjoy?"

The Pu is simply the name of another river. "Hao Pu Pavilion" became a common name for a pavilion overlooking water: there is one in the Liu Garden in Suzhou.

84 The *Mencius* (IV.A.8) records a children's rhyme: "When the water of the Canglang is clear-oh, I can wash my chin-strap. When the water of the Canglang is muddy-oh, I can wash my feet." According to Mencius, Confucius interpreted this to mean that one's behavior, like the water's condition, will attract the appropriate treatment from others, and thus wickedness will lead inevitably to destruction. There is a garden in Suzhou known as the Canglang Pavilion (Canglang Ting), on the edge of a canal; it was founded in 1044.

85 Cao Xuan literally means "Drafting the Mystery." It was the name of a pavilion built when Yang Xiong (Yang Ziyun, 53 BC–18 AD) of the Han dynasty was writing a draft of his *Classic of the Great Mystery* (*Tai Xuan Jing*), a philosophical work modeled on the *Book of Changes* (*Yi Jing*) and emphasizing the power of the laws of Nature. Sima Guang (note 24) wrote a commentary on the book.

86 For Lu Ban and Lu Yun see note 30. To wield one's axe outside Lu Ban's door is a proverbial expression meaning to show off in front of an expert.

87 The building which I have rendered as a "chapel" is one devoted to Buddhist worship or Confucian self-cultivation (thus it can also be described as a study or studio).

88 The *Book of Shang* (also known as the *Classic of History*) is China's earliest historical text and one of the Confucian classics, containing records of the Shang (different character) and Zhou dynasties.

The *Zuo Chronicle* is a commentary on the *Annals of the Spring and Autumn Period* (recording the events of 722-454 BC), supposedly written by Zuo Qiuming, and forming another of the Confucian classics. It probably dates from the early Warring States period (fifth century BC).

The *Selection of Literature* (*Wen Xuan*) was a collection of writings from the Qin, Han, Three Kingdoms, Qi and Liang periods, put together by a member of the Liang royal family. A commentary was added in the Tang dynasty by Li Shan (?–689).

The relevance of these quotations is not clear; it seems that Ji Cheng has nothing much to say about "living-rooms" so he takes the opportunity for this display of arcane learning.

89 The *Explanation of Names* (*Shi Ming*) was an early dictionary compiled in the Han dynasty.

90 The *Analytical Dictionary of Characters* (*Shuo Wen Jie Zi*) is another Han dynasty dictionary.

The *Er Ya* was the earliest Chinese dictionary or work concentrating exclusively on explaining the meanings of words. It was compiled by early Han scholars from records of the Zhou and Han dynasties. It later became regarded as one of the Confucian classics because of its value in understanding the early literature.

91 The logic of this paragraph is as obscure in the original as it is in translation.

92 The Unicorn Building was constructed by Emperor Wu of Han (reigned 140–87 BC) and used by Emperor Xuan (reigned 74–49 BC) to hold the portraits of eleven worthy officials. The appearance of the Chinese unicorn (*qilin*) is associated with the presence of a sage.

The Lingyan (literally "Soaring through the Mist") Building was built for the same purpose by the Tang emperor Taizong (Li Shimin, reigned 626–649), in imitation of the earlier building.

93 Sikong Tu (Sikong Biaosheng, 837–908) was a late Tang recluse. A gloomy character, he called himself "The Recluse who Endures Disgrace." His Xiu Xiu Pavilion contained portraits of distinguished officials and scholars of the high Tang period.

94 "Rectangular with one curved side": this actually refers to the shape of an ancient jade implement, the *gui*, which is generally rectangular with one side either curved or pointed, i.e.

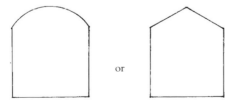

95 The character *xuan* (gallery) is written with the *che* (cart or carriage) radical, so it must originally have had some connection with carriages. The phrase "spacious and lofty" is *xuan xuan yu ju*, written with the same *xuan* character.

96 Ji Cheng refers, of course, not to the letter S but to the character *zhi* 之.

97 The Wu Garden was in Luanjiang (Yizheng County, Jiangsu), and was apparently the garden which Ji Cheng designed for Secretary Wang Shiheng (see Author's Preface). Ruan Dacheng mentions in his introduction that it was a visit to the Wu Garden that first aroused his interest in landscape gardening.

The plan, or perhaps the decoration, of the walkway presumably suggested a formal "cloud" pattern:

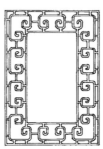

98 The Sweet Dew Temple (Gan Lu Si) is on Beigu Hill outside the present-day city of Zhenjiang. The temple is supposed to have been founded in the Three Kingdoms period by Sun Hao, Marquis of Wucheng (ruled 264–280); this is of course much later than the time that Lu Ban (see note 30) was supposed to have lived. When Ji Cheng says that he saw "several spans" of the Gaoxia Walkway, he presumably means that this was all that survived in his time.

99 I can find no explanation for this curious term.

100 The pictures are hung along the line of either row of inner pillars; the absence of the line of "backbone" pillars (directly below the roof ridge) means that one can step further back to admire the pictures.

101 The absence of a pillar (the outermost backbone pillar) in the middle of the end wall means that the end wall can be knocked through in the middle to make a window or door.

102 "Moulded corners" are literally "ground" or "milled" corners. It appears that this term is used with reference to smaller buildings, while the term "drawn-up corners" is used for larger, more formal buildings, although the two terms really refer to the same thing, the characteristic upturned corners of the eaves.

103 Partly for aesthetic reasons, since these two types of small, whimsically shaped pavilions are intended to give a rustic impression, and partly for practical reasons since thatch would be much lighter on such comparatively flimsy structures than would a tiled roof. The weight of a tiled roof (tiles, planking and mortar) could be as much as 400 kg per square meter.

104 The *Later Han History* (*Hou Han Shu*) tells the following story:

> A man of Runan, the eldest son of the Fei family, was an official of the city market. There was an old fellow who hung up a gourd at one end of the market, where he sold medicines. Whenever the market closed, he always jumped into the gourd, and disappeared before the eyes of the market people. Only Mr Fei observed him carefully from an upper storey and realized that the old man was something out of the ordinary, so he went repeatedly to pay his respects to him. Then Fei went with him into the gourd and saw a wonderful jade palace, with delicious food and wine laid out in abundance. When they had finished drinking together, they came out of the gourd and went upstairs, where the old man bowed to Fei and said, "I am an immortal and have been doing penance for my past sins; now that I have been of service to you I must depart."

Magic flasks or gourds often occur in Chinese tales of the supernatural and they are particularly associated with Daoist sages and immortals. Lü Dongbin, one of the Eight Immortals, is always depicted carrying a gourd.

105 Water-caltrop: *trapa natans*. The flowers are white. The fruit, which can be two-, three-, or four-pointed, is similar in texture to a water-chestnut and is edible. Caltrops are particularly popular as a vegetable dish in Zhejiang province; they have a pleasant, nutty taste.

106 Presumably because the two faces of the door, held apart by the frame, give it something of the structure of a drum (see figs *a* and *b* in margin).

107 For water-caltrop, see note 105.

108 The "willow-leaf" shape is in fact simply a long, narrow rectangle. Presumably it was the length that led to the name "never-ending window."

109 The Chinese inch (*cun*) is approximately equivalent to 1.3 imperial inches.

110 Calligraphy was an almost exclusively male activity, just as embroidery was a female one.

111 What this seems to mean is that the "belts" can be placed at either the top or the bottom, or both, of the taller window, in such a way that the middle section of the taller window is the same size as, and on a line

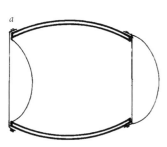

a

drum

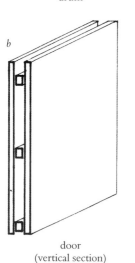

b

door
(vertical section)

with the smaller (lower) window, e.g.:

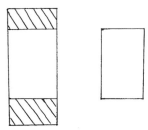

112 Cracked ice (or breaking ice): as well as being intrinsically attractive and pleasingly asymmetrical, this pattern recalls the words of Lao Zi in the *Dao De Jing*, where the sage is described as "falling apart like thawing ice; thick like the uncarved block" (*Dao De Jing* xv.35). This implies that the sage can adapt to all the changes of Nature.

113 This avoids monotony and gives balance and stability to the pattern as the bottom is "heavier" and the top "lighter." The effect can be seen in the diagram.

114 When the window is propped open, the middle leaf can be folded back to rest on the upper leaf (see fig. *c* in margin).

115 As an Indian mystic symbol, the connection of the swastika with Buddhism is obvious, and no doubt this pattern would appear out of place in a non-Buddhist context. However, it is not clear what Ji Cheng's objection to concentric squares is; perhaps simply that this seemed a very old-fashioned design. In summer, beds were used which were specially constructed for coolness, normally from bamboo; I do not know why concentric squares should be thought appropriate for their decoration.

116 Seal characters are a particular style of writing developed before the unification of the Chinese script in the Qin dynasty and later usually used for carving names on seals. The style is angular and therefore quite suitable for rendering in woodwork. The sort of characters which one would expect to appear in a balustrade are "happiness," "long life" and so on, which the literati would no doubt consider ineffably vulgar.

117 This could mean a balustrade one foot (*chi*) high (a Chinese foot, or *chi* is ten *cun*, i.e. about thirteen inches) or a balustrade like a carpenter's square, also called *chi* (cf. diagram IV.123).

118 When placed outside a doorway, presumably the balustrade is between the pillars of the verandah, and the low height is used in order not to impede the sense of freedom enjoyed on stepping out of doors. The balustrade could no doubt easily be stepped over, especially by people used to avoiding tripping over the high door-sills of Chinese buildings.

119 "Leaves of jade" refers either to plantain or to bamboo. Windows could be "glazed" with silk rather than paper. The image is of a round silk fan with a jade rim.

120 This is another reference to the kingdom within the magic gourd (see note 104).

121 The sound of the breeze blowing through the bamboos is being compared to the music of the sheng, a sort of Chinese mouth-organ whose nearest Western equivalent (visual if not aural) is the pan-pipes.

122 Presumably the lower side of the lintel was curved to form the arch.

123 The dowels at a 45° angle are in the facing bricks, not the wood:

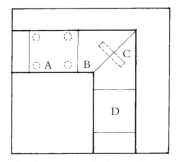

B bricks covering wooden lintel
A dowels attaching brick to wood
C dowel at 45° angle attaching brick to brick
D bricks

124 This shape is described as another type of *gui* or jade implement (see note 94).

125 Lotuses, as a symbol of purity (they "rise from the mud but are undefiled"), are associated with the Buddha. Buddhas and Bodhisatvas are usually depicted sitting or standing on a lotus. The Lotus Sutra is one of the classic texts of Buddhism.

　　The *ruyi* ("as you wish") scepter was a symbol of success, often presented to officials as a sign of honor. The shape of the end suggests a lotus petal and it must originally have had some religious (Buddhist) significance.

　　The bodhi-tree (*borassus flabelliformis* or fan-palm), which grows in India and South-East Asia, was the

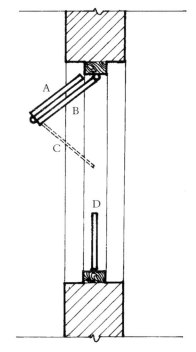

A middle leaf
B upper leaf
C prop (lower end resting on window frame)
D lower leaf

tree under which Gautama Buddha achieved enlightenment. The early Buddhist scriptures were written on bodhi-leaves.

126 Vase for casting lots: vases of this shape are used to hold the sticks (originally stalks of the milfoil, *achillea sibirica*) used for divination. Each stick has a number or other symbol marked on it. The person wishing to consult the oracle holds the vase in both hands and shakes it until one stick falls out. The number or symbol on that stick is then looked up in a book such as the *Book of Changes* (*Yi Jing*) and the entry is interpreted to suggest an answer to the inquirer's problem or question.

127 Hollyhock: the word *kui* used by Ji Cheng can mean a number of different plants including the sunflower. This design looks most like a hollyhock to me.

Begonia: for some reason dictionaries always define the *haitang* as *malus spectabilis* (Chinese flowering apple or cherry-apple). In fact it can also mean the begonia, as this diagram confirms.

128 Gardenia: *gardenia jasminoides*, cape-jasmine.

129 What Ji Cheng seems to be suggesting is that where the ground falls away and makes it difficult or unattractive to construct a rectangular building, one should construct a building whose outside shape is irregular but whose inner form is a regular rectangle, as a result of the uneven thickness of the walls, e.g.:

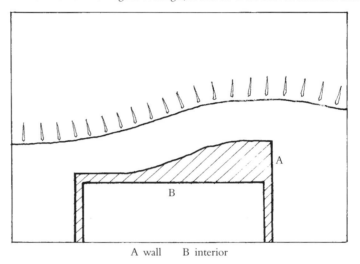

A wall   B interior

130 I understand from Professor Chen Congzhou that paper-pulp is still a normal ingredient in whitewash for walls.

131 The screen wall inside a main gate is also known as the spirit wall. Because evil spirits can only travel in a straight line they are unable to negotiate the screen wall and so cannot enter the house. The more immediate purpose, however, is to baffle inquisitive outsiders. These screen walls could be very elaborately decorated.

"Hanging corners" means that the bricks were laid with two corners pointing straight up and down, to form a diamond pattern:

(elevation)

132 "Flying eaves" are the characteristic upturned edges of Chinese roofs which are used on walls as well as on buildings.

133 Openwork: the Chinese term is *lou zhuan*; bricks with holes in them. This refers to the laying of bricks or tiles in a wall with spaces between them to form a pattern. The use of such "semitransparent" walls in Chinese gardens is a common device to intrigue the viewer and draw the eye from an enclosed space to a wider vista.

134 The reason for avoiding patterns such as "strings of cash" and "heaped ingots" is not only that they are old-fashioned and hackneyed but that their association with money makes them too vulgar. Even fish can be associated with money through the common pun on "fish" (*yu*) and "abundance" (*yu*).

135 For Huang rocks, see page 115 and note 188.

136 The mixture of lime and tung oil forms a sort of putty or mortar. Tung oil, the oil of *aleurite fordii* or *aleurite montana,* was an important ingredient in paint manufacture and used to be one of China's major exports.

137 "Cracked ice" here suggests a sort of vertical crazy-paving effect.

138 Ji Cheng does not explain why these different patterns are appropriate in different places.

139 Sichuan province (here referred to by Ji Cheng under its ancient name of Shu) was famous for the weaving of silk brocade.

The Terrace of the King of Qin was famous for its magnificence in ancient times.

140 Lotuses blooming under one's feet of course refers to the design of the paving. There is also a literary reference to the *Southern History* which describes how Marquis Donghun of Qi made his concubine Lady Pan walk over a pattern of lotuses and exclaimed "A lotus blossoms at every step!" Women's bound feet were described as "golden lotuses" but no allusion to this seems intended here.

141 A reference to the famous "Ode on the Goddess of the River Luo" by Cao Zhi (192–232): "Sometimes gathering bright pearls, sometimes collecting kingfisher feathers" and to a line by Du Fu (712–770): "As the fair lady gathers kingfisher feathers, the spring greets her." The gleaming blue feathers of the kingfisher (*halcyon smyrnensis*; in Chinese the turquoise or lapis lazuli bird) were inlaid in jewellery.

142 The *Later Han History* refers to a proverb, "An unsuccessful painting of a tiger ends up looking like a dog," to describe the bathetic results of attempts at grandeur.

143 "Crazy paving": the actual Chinese term is "cracked-ice ground."

144 The word for target is actually "goal" for a ballgame.

145 "Herringbone" is actually the pattern formed from the character for man: *ren* 人 (cf. diagram v.48). I have translated it elsewhere as "zigzags."

"Woven hat pattern": the Chinese term is *dou* pattern. The word *dou* may mean a bushel measure, a scoop or, apparently, a woven hat ("coolie hat"), which seems the most likely translation here judging by the pattern illustrated (diagram v.51).

146 Ji Cheng saves his favorite subjects, mountains and rocks, to the last. These were evidently his real specialty: his descriptions in these sections are much more detailed and thorough than for other topics, there is much less use of contrived "literary" language, and one can feel his enthusiasm.

147 Great Lake rocks fell into different categories depending on their shape and form. "Thin" rocks were like a single pillar sticking up into the air; the surface of "riddled" rocks (*lou*: the same word as the "openwork" walls) was pitted with holes. *Ling-long*, the word translated as "filigree," implies delicate tracery.

148 The altar in a Chinese temple will generally have a tall incense-burner in the middle flanked by a pair of candlesticks and a pair of flower-vases on either side: a symmetrical arrangement which would indeed look out of place in a natural garden.

The hill of knives and tree of swords are recorded as instruments of torture used in the Song dynasty.

149 The Five Ancients is the highest peak of Mount Lu (Lu Shan) in Jiangxi; the peak has the appearance of five old men standing together.

150 "The cat catching mice" was the name of a children's game.

151 Fengdu, a place in Sichuan, was reputedly inhabited by ghosts or by Yama, the King of the Underworld, himself.

152 See note 83.

153 Pines, plum and bamboo are the "three friends in winter" (see note 36). Their addition among the rocks would enhance the impression of looking at an ancient painting. The Huangshan referred to here is the famous mountain in Anhui, a favorite subject of landscape painters.

154 The laws of dynamic balance seem in fact to refer to the way of arranging rocks so that they are steady and will not tip or overbalance, rather than to anything to do with water or hydraulic engineering, as is implied in this passage. Compare "Sharp Peaks" and "Overhanging Cliffs" on pages 109 and 110. A similar concept is referred to in the *Shi Shuo Xin Yu* (*A New Account of Tales of the World*) compiled during the fifth century; this reflects the early development of science in China.

155 "Brush-rest": although the Chinese word is ambiguous, Ji Cheng is evidently thinking not of the frame from which to hang writing-brushes, but of the stand on which to rest them while in use. These stands were often made in the shape of a range of mountains.

156 The meander or serpentine (*qushui*) is an almost essential component of a cultured person's garden. Participants in literary gatherings would sit along the banks of the meander while wine cups were floated down the stream. Each person had to compose and recite an appropriate couplet by the time the next wine cup reached him; if he failed, he had to drink its contents as a forfeit. Such an event would recall the most famous of all such gatherings, the one which took place at the calligrapher Wang Xizhi's Orchid Pavilion (Lan Ting) just outside Shaoxing in Zhejiang, on the third day of the third month in 353. The poems composed on that occasion were collected into a book, to which Wang Xizhi wrote a preface which became

one of the great models of both prose-writing and calligraphy.

157 See "Precipitous Mountains" on page 107.

158 The implication is that the "cliff" down which the waterfall pours is built up against an existing wall. There is evidently a channel along the top of the wall to carry the rain-water which will form the waterfall. It seems that the waterfall can only function when it has been raining. The Song emperor Huizong's park, Gen Yue (see note 162), had a waterfall which had to be primed by coolies carrying the water uphill in buckets.

159 This seems to be a proverbial expression.

160 Tiger Hill was one of the few of Suzhou's famous examples of landscape art which were generally open to the public at this time. The inhabitants of the area were famous for their traditional skill at creating bonsai plants and miniature landscapes.

　　Phoenix Terrace Gate was one of the city gates of Nanjing in the Ming dynasty. The Temple of the Flower Gods was nearby and, like Tiger Hill, it was a center of horticulture and miniature landscapes.

161 The Great Lake is Tai Hu or Lake Tai, in Jiangsu.

162 "Patterned rocks" refers to the "Patterned Rock Convoy" (*Hua Shi Gang*), which brought "strange rocks" from all over the empire, and especially from the Great Lake area, to the capital, Kaifeng, on the orders of the Song emperor Huizong (reigned 1100–1125), who built a large, mountainous park named "Gen Yue, the Mountain of Longevity" partly for geomantic purposes. The extortionate methods of his rock-collectors were supposed to have contributed to the fall of the Song dynasty.

163 The fact that it was possible to choose rocks for a garden from illustrated catalogues indicates how advanced the rock business was in Ji Cheng's time.

164 The Master of the Cloud Forest was the pen-name of the painter Ni Zan (Ni Yuanzhen), who lived from either 1301 or 1306 to 1374, at the end of the Yuan dynasty. He came of a wealthy family from Wuxi in Jiangsu, but to escape the confusion of the last years of the Yuan he sold his estates and lived a wandering life around the Great Lake, eventually being converted from Buddhism to Daoism. He specialized in painting landscapes (usually uninhabited) and was influenced by Ji Cheng's idols Jing Hao and Guan Tong. He was particularly famous for his rendering of craggy rocks. He also did ink paintings of bamboos, and described his own style in the words: "My leisurely brush scrawls away, and I don't try to achieve a likeness." He was also a poet and calligrapher.

　　Zijiu is Huang Gongwang (see note 41). Ni Zan, Huang Gongwang, Wu Zhen and Wang Meng were known as the Four Great Masters of the Yuan dynasty.

165 This (slightly strained) parallelism indicates that Ji Cheng felt that there was a lot in common between people and rocks: both are more sturdy and adaptable than plants or trees. For the Confucian, the contemplation of rocks was an aid to the cultivation of human character.

166 See note 45.

167 These are all rock-collectors' technical terms.

168 Ma'anshan (Horse Saddle Mountain) was also known as Kunshan and gave its name to Kunshan County, Jiangsu province. The mountain is also known as Jade Peak because of the whiteness of the rock.

169 Iris (*qisun*): *iris sibirica*.

170 Yixing is the place in Jiangsu famous for its "violet sand" pottery. Master Zhang's Cave is to the south-east of the county seat. Master Zhang was Zhang Daoling (34–156), a Daoist adept of the Han dynasty, who came from the Jiangsu area and was supposed to have practiced his arts in this cave.

　　Shanjuan's Temple is also known as Shanjuan's Cave; it is to the south-west of Yixing County seat. Shanjuan was a legendary ancient hermit. *Zhuang Zi* records the following story:

> Shun tried to cede the empire to Shanjuan, but Shanjuan said, "I stand in the midst of space and time. On winter days I dress in skins and furs, on summer days, in vine-cloth and hemp. In spring I plough and plant—this gives my body the labor and exercise it needs; in fall I harvest and store away—this gives my form the leisure and sustenance it needs. When the sun comes up, I work; when the sun goes down, I rest. I wander free and easy between heaven and earth, and my mind has found all that it could wish for. What use would I have for the empire? What a pity that you don't understand me!" In the end he would not accept, but went away, entering deep into the mountains, and no-one ever knew where he had gone.
>
> [Burton Watson's translation, with alterations]

171 Dragon Pool (Longtan) is now in the outskirts of the city of Nanjing. Seven Stars Convent (Qi Xing Guan), Hillmouth (Shankou) and Granary Head (Cangtou) were all small places around Longtan.

172 Green Dragon Hill (Qing Long Shan) is outside the Zhongshan Gate of Nanjing and is known for its stone quarries and lime kilns.

173 See note 148.

174 This Suzhou is not the famous city of gardens, but a place in Anhui, written with a different character. Lingbi County (the name means "magic jade") now belongs to Fengyang district. Ancient Chinese court music made much use of stone chimes. They were usually in the shape of a carpenter's square, and were hung on a large wooden frame.

175 The text reads "lodestone" or "magnetite" rather than porcelain, but the characters are interchangeable, and the abrasiveness of powdered porcelain seems more relevant here.

176 The *Classic of History* is the same as the *Book of Shang* (see note 88).

The stones from which the chimes were made had the appearance of floating in the water of the river. The Si River rises from four (*si*) springs in Shandong.

177 Da Xian Mountain is in the southern outskirts of the present-day city of Zhenjiang. It is near Zhenjiang's Huangshan.

178 Ningguo County is to the south-east of Xuancheng County in Anhui, in the region of Wuhu. This area is also the source of the famous "xuan paper" used by Chinese artists.

179 The plum-rain season comes in the fourth and fifth months of the lunar calendar, when the plums (or apricots) ripen. The weather is notoriously damp at this time in the Jiangnan area and everything indoors grows mildew; in fact the Chinese words for mildew and plum sound exactly alike (*mei*), so the original name for this time of year may have been the less poetic "mildew-rain season."

It is not made clear why the rocks have to be washed clean at this particular season; it is probably simply because this is the only time of the year when sufficiently heavy rain can be guaranteed.

180 These rocks have protuberances on them which are supposed to look like horses' teeth.

181 The place referred to as Jiangzhou is now the city of Jiujiang in Jiangxi, on the Yangtze River. Hukou is situated at the northern tip of the Poyang Lake, where it connects with the Yangtze, hence the name, which means Lake Mouth.

182 Su Dongpo or Su Shi (1037–1101) was one of the greatest Song dynasty writers, as well as an able administrator. Originally from Sichuan, he graduated as a *jinshi* in about 1060. He was at various times an official at the Song court and also governor of a number of cities, including Hangzhou. He was responsible for the construction of one of the causeways (now known as the Su Causeway) across Hangzhou's famous West Lake. As well as being a writer he was an accomplished calligrapher, who also enjoyed painting bamboos and rocks. He was also a rock-collector.

183 Jiuhua Mountain is in Anhui. The name means "Nine Blossoms"; it has nine peaks and the whole mountain resembles a lotus blossom.

Su Dongpo (see note 182) records in his introduction to the poem "Jiuhua in a pint pot":

> Li Zhengchen from Hukou had in his collection a remarkable rock called "Nine Peaks," of delicate sinuous tracery like the lattice of a window. I wanted to buy it for a hundred gold pieces, to match my "Chouchi Rocks." However, just then I had to move south, so I had no time to do this. I named it "Jiuhua in a pint pot" and wrote a poem as a record of it.

The line quoted by Ji Cheng is the last line of this poem. On Su Dongpo's return to Hukou eight years later he found that the rock had been bought by somebody else.

184 Yingzhou is the present Yingde County in Guangdong. Su Dongpo's "Chouchi Rocks" (note 183) were Ying rocks; he named them after Mount Chouchi in Gansu which was important in Daoist mythology.

185 Zhang Liang (Zhang Zifang, died 189 BC) acted as a strategist for Liu Bang (256 or 247–195 BC), founder of the Han dynasty (206 BC–220 AD). After co-operating with the Chu leader Xiang Yu in the overthrow of the Qin dynasty, Liu Bang fought against Xiang Yu in a war which lasted for five years, finally defeating him in 202 BC. When the Han army had surrounded Xiang Yu's forces, Zhang Liang gave the order to sing Chu folk-songs; Xiang Yu and his army thus thought that an enormous number of their own people had gone over to the other side, and were totally demoralized.

186 Lake Chao or Jiao is in the present Chao County, Anhui, near the provincial capital, Hefei.

187 Ji Cheng refers to Yangzhou in Jiangsu by its old name of Weiyang.

188 Although strictly speaking the term "Huang rocks" should refer to rocks from Huangshan (whichever Huangshan this may mean), it is generally used to refer to rocks which are of a fairly regular shape, with comparatively flat surfaces, by contrast with the fantastic forms of Great Lake rocks.

189 Huangshan: this is not of course the famous Huangshan in Anhui; Changzhou is in Jiangsu. Caishi is now part of the city of Ma'anshan in Anhui.

190 "Grey bones": the color word actually used by Ji Cheng is *qing* which can mean black, blue, green or grey depending on the object it refers to; in fact the meaning is something like the heraldic term "proper." I have used the word grey because stones usually are grey. I suppose "grey bones" means darker striations in the rock.

191 The word I have translated "bushel" is actually a "picul" or about 130lbs.

Although the Chinese invented coin and paper money at an early date, the Chinese economy remained largely a barter economy for a long time, and to some extent still is. Rice was often used as a substitute for money, and in imperial China officials' salaries were paid largely in grain (as they were also under the Republic, when runaway inflation made money almost worthless).

192 Jinchuan is present-day Xiaolinghe in Jin County, Liaoning.

193 See note 162.

194 Luhe County is now part of Nanjing municipality, and Spiritual Dwelling Cliff (Ling Ju Yan) is generally known as Spirit Cliff Mountain (Ling Yan Shan).

Nanjing's agate pebbles, known as rain flower pebbles (*yu hua shi*) because they come from a place where it once rained flowers as a famous Buddhist was expounding the sutras, are much prized for their natural beauty. Scholars would keep them on their desks, often in a bowl of water to bring out the colors, for contemplation.

195 Du Wan (Du Jiyang), a twelfth-century descendant of the great Tang poet Du Fu, wrote a work called *The Cloud Forest Catalogue of Rocks* (he called himself "Hermit of the Cloud Forest"), which is the first extant work dealing exclusively with the subject of rocks and rock-collecting. Edward Schafer, who has published a summary translation of the work with notes and introduction (*Tu Wan's Stone Catalogue of Cloudy Forest*, Berkeley and Los Angeles, University of California Press, 1961), believes that Du Wan may have been one of the officials who collected rocks for the Emperor Huizong's great collection, and that the *Catalogue of Rocks*, though not a formal catalogue of the imperial collection, may be based upon it. At any rate Du Wan was evidently familiar with the imperial collection. He also knew the collection of Su Dongpo (see note 182), who was a friend of his father (another rock-collector). Du Wan describes 114 different types of rock in considerable and factual detail. Some of Ji Cheng's descriptions follow Du Wan's. Because Ji Cheng confines himself to describing rocks which he himself has actually used in garden design, the rocks which he mentions cover a much more limited geographical area than Du Wan's.

196 The Angel of the Flowers, or the immortal among flowers, was the begonia (*haitang*) according to the Tang writer Jia Dan (730–805), because of its exceptionally beautiful color.

197 An old text quoted in relation to a poem by Du Fu explains that "drunkards refer to clear wine as the Saint and opaque wine as the Sage."

The Prime Minister in the Mountains was a celebrated scholar and Daoist recluse in the time of the Southern dynasties, named Tao Hongjing (456–536). Frequent gifts from the court failed to lure him from his mountain retreat, but whenever any major event took place, the court would always send to ask his advice, hence his nickname.

198 Pan Yue (247–300) was a poet and court official of the Jin dynasty.

Qu Yuan was the reputed author of the pre-Han *Songs of Chu* (*Chu Ci*). His suicide by drowning in protest at the corruption of the court is still commemorated by the Dragon Boat Festival. The poems, which are of shamanistic origin, contain many names of fragrant herbs and flowering plants which are interpreted allegorically as the virtues which Qu Yuan upheld in the face of the evil all around him.

Neither poet's name is mentioned by Ji Cheng but the allusions are clear.

199 The magical and ritual associations of the swing, known to the ancient Greeks, seem to have been recognized by the Chinese also.

200 Fuxi is the Chinese Adam. The human race sprang from the union of Fuxi with his sister and consort Nü Wa. Fuxi taught mankind to make nets and to hunt and fish. He also discovered or invented the Eight Trigrams, the mystic symbols of ancient Chinese belief.

Tao Yuanming (see notes 54 and 56) wrote that when he lay beneath his north-facing window in the summer, enjoying the cool breeze, he could imagine himself to be back in the golden age of Fuxi.

201 This refers to a line from Tao Yuanming's poem "Returning": "I lean by the southern window to express my exalted emotions." For Tao Yuanming, see notes 54, 56, 200.

202 "Northern shutters": this refers to the passage of Tao Yuanming paraphrased in note 200.

203 It was believed that the first leaf fell from the phoenix-tree (*firmiana simplex*) on the first day of autumn, and it continued to drop one leaf a day until the arrival of winter.

204 "Rub your eyes": the original actually says "scratch your head," which does not sound so vulgar in Chinese. This is a quotation from the *Book of Songs* (*Shi Jing*): "Loving her but not seeing her, I scratch my head and wander irresolute."

"Wonder at the clear sky": a reference to Su Dongpo's lines: "How often is the moon so bright? I raise my wine and question the clear sky." For Su Dongpo, see note 182.

The next sentence alludes to the great Tang poet Li Bai (701–762), better known in the West, through Arthur Waley's translations, as Li Po: "I raise my glass and invite the bright moon, who, with my shadow, makes three of us."

205 The heavenly fragrance is that of *osmanthus fragrans* (*gui hua,* often translated as cassia). The osmanthus flowers in the autumn and so it is particularly associated with that season. It is also associated with the moon: there is an osmanthus tree on the moon, under which a hare mixes the elixir of life.

206 This sentence does not quote but recalls the words of poets such as Tao Yuanming (see note 54) and Su Dongpo (see note 182), who frequently refer to buying wine and drinking with their country neighbors. The money, presumably strings of cash, is tied to one's staff as a way of carrying it to the local wineshop (ancient Chinese clothes did not have pockets).

207 This is an allusion to a poem by Gao Qi (1336–1374): "Snow fills the mountains as the gentleman of high ideals lies at ease; the moon shines down through the forest as the fair lady approaches."

There was a legend that once when the hillsides were covered with snow, Zhao Shixiong met a beautiful woman in the woods at dusk. She was plainly dressed and wearing light make-up. As Zhao Shixiong talked to her, a wonderful fragrance enveloped him, so he knocked on the door of a wineshop and had a drink with her. After a short time a boy in green appeared, and sang and danced. Zhao Shixiong got drunk and fell asleep. After a long time, when it was already light in the east, he saw that he was under a great plum tree, with its pale green leaves rustling in the wind, and the light of the setting moon slanting through the braches.

A commentary on the biography of Yuan An (first century) in the *Later Han History* also records the following story:

> Once at a time of heavy snow, when it was piled up over ten feet high above the ground, the Governor of Luoyang went out on his rounds. He saw that people from every household had come out to sweep away the snow. There was also a beggar who had gone to Yuan An's gate but had seen that there was no pathway cleared, so he said Yuan An must be dead. The governor ordered people to clear the snow and entered the house, where he saw Yuan An reclining on his bed. When he asked him why he hadn't gone out, Yuan An replied, "In heavy snow everyone goes to bed; I didn't like to disturb people."

208 The stream of Yan was where Wang Ziyou went to visit Dai Andao. A fourth-century work, the *Forest of Tales* (*Yu Lin*), tells the story as follows:

> Wang Ziyou lived at Shanyin [present-day Shaoxing in Zhejiang]. During a heavy snowfall at night, he opened up his house and called for wine. Looking at the gleaming whiteness all around he intoned the poem "Summoning the Hermit." Then suddenly he thought of Dai Andao. At that time Dai was at Yan Stream, so Wang got into a boat and set off. It took him all night to get there, but as soon as he reached the gate he turned back. When he was asked why, he replied: "I went there because I felt in the mood; when the mood was over I came back; there was no need actually to call on Dai."

This story is often illustrated in literati painting. The scholar class valued (and still does) the immediacy of feeling shown by Wang Ziyou (Wang Huizhi, the son of the calligrapher Wang Xizhi; see note 156).

209 See note 69. The original appears to make a comparison with the Dangs' *tea.* It was of course the Tao household, rather than the Dangs, who went in for tea-tasting, but an allusion to the surname Tao would be much less clear.

210 The turmoil of current events being avoided by Ji Cheng was the crumbling of the Ming dynasty.

211 An allusion to the story of someone who, when asked by an aspiring hermit friend for one million pieces of silver to buy a mountain as a retreat, immediately handed over the money.

212 Ji Cheng refers to Tao Yuanming's famous "Record of the Peach Blossom Spring," the description of an idyllic utopian valley, hidden away from the turmoil of the world. Ji Cheng says that he would have been glad to live just near such a place, not even in it.

213 The strategist Zhuge Liang is one of the leading characters in the early Chinese historical novel, *The Romance of the Three Kingdoms.* He is also a much admired figure in many traditional Chinese operas, as he thinks up one brilliant scheme after another to defeat the dastardly Cao Cao.

Di Renjie (630–700) had a difficult career under Empress Wu Zetian. Interestingly, he was at one point demoted to being magistrate of Pengze, a job which Tao Yuanming had held some centuries earlier. Di Renjie was renowned for speaking his mind fearlessly during the reign of the formidable Empress, who held the throne (the only woman in Chinese history ever to do so) from 690 to 705. In fact Empress Wu Zetian seems to have been an able ruler, but has received a very bad press from later Confucian scholars not only because she was a woman but also because, as an ardent Buddhist, she promoted Buddhism as the state religion and tried to restrict the power of the Confucians.

214 A reference to Tao Yuanming's poem "Putting the Blame on my Sons" (406):

> White hair covers my temples,

My muscles are no longer springy,
And although I have five sons,
Not one of them cares for paper and brush.
Ah-shu is already sixteen,
But for laziness he has no equal.
Ah-xuan does his best to learn,
But has no affinity for literature.
Yong and Duan are thirteen,
But can't add six and seven.
Tongzi has nine years behind him,
But only hunts for pears and chestnuts.
If such is my fate from heaven,
Bring me the "thing in the cup."

215 Sima Guang wrote this essay while living in retirement at Luoyang, where he spent fifteen years from 1071. It was also at this time that he wrote or edited the *Comprehensive Mirror to Aid in Government*, a task which he completed in 1084. In 1086, he was recalled to the court as Prime Minister, but died later that year at the age of 67.

There are two rather charming stories attached to Sima Guang's occupancy of the garden. One relates that he had an underground chamber constructed to escape the heat of summer (he does not mention this in the essay, so it may have been in his residence elsewhere in Luoyang, rather than in the garden); another distinguished resident of the city, Wang Gongchen, had a particularly high tower in his garden, and everyone remarked on the difference between Wang ascending his skyscraper and Sima burrowing into the earth.

The historian Liu Anshi, one of Sima Guang's closest associates, who spent about ten years in Luoyang with Sima, relates another story as follows:

> The Garden of Solitary Delight was the least pretentious of all the gardens in Luoyang, but because of Sima Guang's reputation, everyone made a point of visiting it when it was open to the public in spring. It was the custom in Luoyang that the caretaker of a garden, when it closed to the public, would divide the tips which he had received from visitors with the garden's owner. In one day the caretaker, surnamed Lü, received ten thousand strings of cash, and hauled it along to hand over to Lord Sima. When he asked why, the caretaker explained about the local custom. Lord Sima said, "The money is yours; you can take it away." The caretaker kept trying to hand it over, until Lord Sima became quite angry. Eventually he did take it away, turning round as he went to say, "Only Duanming would refuse the money." ["Scholar of the Duanming Hall" was one of Sima Guang's honorary titles.] Ten days or so later, Lord Sima noticed that a new pavilion had been built among the trees in the garden, and when he made enquiries he learnt that it had been put up by the man from whom he had refused to take the ten thousand cash.

216 It was customary to open an essay or other literary work by quoting from ancient authorities such as Confucius. The philosopher Mencius (fourth century BC) was Confucius' greatest successor; the record of his teachings became one of the great Confucian classics. Master Yan (Yan Hui or Yan Ziyuan) was the most brilliant of Confucius' immediate disciples; he lived in poverty and died young. This quotation, like the saying of Confucius before it, is taken from *The Analects*.

217 As a young man, Sima Guang had written a book called *The Pedant*. At the time of writing this essay, he was in his fifties, and therefore refers to himself as "the Old Pedant."

218 Luoyang, in Henan province, was one of the earliest seats of Chinese civilization; it was the capital of the Northern Wei dynasty (fourth to fifth centuries) and of the Empress Wu Zetian, as well as being an alternative capital to Chang'an throughout the Tang dynasty. It was always a great center of Buddhist culture.

219 Apparently Sima Guang wished to become "familiar with their appearance" in order to be able to paint these flowers, since the quantity seems too small for medicinal use.

220 Sima Guang seems to have communed with these "wise men" and "worthy folk" through their books only; he does not appear to be referring to personal encounters.

221 This criticism (if it was really made) may have been motivated by political enmity, since at the time when Sima Guang was living at Luoyang he had retired from the court in opposition to the economic reforms of Wang Anshi. However, despite the emperor's support for Wang Anshi, Sima Guang was not personally out of favor; it was the emperor who had put him in charge of producing the *Comprehensive Mirror to Aid in Government*.

DATES OF THE CHINESE DYNASTIES

Xia Dynasty（夏）... 2070–1600 BC
Shang Dynasty（商）.. 1600–1046 BC
Zhou Dynasty（周）... 1046–256 BC
    Western Zhou Dynasty（西周）.. 1046–771 BC
    Eastern Zhou Dynasty（东周）... 770–256 BC
        Spring and Autumn Period（春秋）................................ 770–476 BC
        Warring States Period（战国）...................................... 475–221 BC
Qin Dynasty（秦）.. 221–206 BC
Han Dynasty（汉）... 206 BC–220 AD
    Western Han Dynasty（西汉）... 206 BC–25 AD
    Eastern Han Dynasty（东汉）.. 25–220
Three Kingdoms（三国）.. 220–280
    Wei（魏）.. 220–265
    Shu Han（蜀）... 221–263
    Wu（吴）... 222–280
Jin Dynasty（晋）... 265–420
    Western Jin Dynasty（西晋）... 265–316
    Eastern Jin Dynasty（东晋）... 317–420
Northern and Southern Dynasties（南北朝）............................ 420–589
    Southern Dynasties（南朝）.. 420–589
    Liang Dynasty（梁）... 502–557
    Northern Dynasties（北朝）... 439–581
Sui Dynasty（隋）.. 581–618
Tang Dynasty（唐）... 618–907
Five Dynasties and Ten Kingdoms（五代十国）...................... 907–960
    Five Dynasties（五代）.. 907–960
    Ten Kingdoms（十国）.. 902–979
Song Dynasty（宋）... 960–1279
    Northern Song Dynasty（北宋）....................................... 960–1127
    Southern Song Dynasty（南宋）....................................... 1127–1279
Liao Dynasty（辽）.. 916–1125
Jin Dynasty（金）.. 1115–1234
Xixia Dynasty (or Tangut)（西夏）... 1038–1227
Yuan Dynasty（元）... 1279–1368
Ming Dynasty（明）... 1368–1644
    The more noteworthy Ming reign-periods were:
    Hongwu.. 1368–1399
    Yongle.. 1403–1425
    Xuande... 1426–1436
    Jiajing.. 1522–1566
    Wanli... 1573–1620
    Chongzhen (last Ming emperor)...................................... 1628–1644
Qing Dynasty（清）... 1644–1911

INDEX

"Three Auspicious Things" 45, 126n.36
"Three Friends in Winter" 126n.36, 133n.153
Three Kingdoms 121, 129n.88, 130n.98
Three Pines Zhu see Zhu Sansong
Tian Shan see Celestial Mountains
Tiger Hill 111, 134n.160
tile 94, 99, 101, 102, 103, 130n.103, 132n.133
ting 70, 125n.33
Tongli 19, 124n.13
torrent, mountain torrent 45, 48, 53, 110
tower 45, 48, 57, 59, 60, 65, 66, 69, 74, 75, 106, 107, 109, 128n.82, 138n.215
trapa bispinosa 127n.59
trapa natans 127n.59, 130n.105
tree 15, 17, 18, 19, 22, 23, 24, 26, 31, 33, 37, 41, 42, 45, 46, 47, 48, 49, 51, 52, 55, 57, 59, 69, 106, 107, 110, 112, 113, 114, 116, 117, 120, 123, 124n.1, 126n.47, 134n.165, 137n.205, 138n.215
Tree God see God of Spring
"tree of swords" 104, 114, 133n.148
tree-peony 127n.55
trellis 49
Tu Wan's Stone Catalogue of Cloudy Forest 136n.195
Tui Si Cao Tang 19
Tui Si Yuan 19
Tushan 116

underground chamber 138n.215
Unicorn Building 69, 129n.92

valley 15, 17, 31, 35, 48, 52, 101, 104, 106, 118, 121, 137n.212
"vanilla pod" pattern 102
vase 94, 95, 104, 114, 132n.126, 133n.148
vaulting 70, 71, 72, 73, 74, 76
vegetable garden 31, 49
verandah 45, 49, 64, 65, 70, 71, 99, 120, 131n.118
view 12, 15, 18, 22, 23, 35, 37, 41, 42, 43, 45, 47, 49, 54, 55, 60, 65, 93, 106, 107, 120, 123, 125n.33, 128nn.75, 79
Vimalakirti 19
vine 120, 134n.170

Waley, Arthur 136n.204
walkway, covered 22, 60, 61, 63, 64, 71, 76, 125n.27
wall 15, 16, 18, 23, 25, 26, 27, 43, 45, 47, 49, 52, 56, 63, 67, 70, 74, 75, 76, 90, 93, 94, 96, 97, 98, 99, 107, 109, 111, 120, 122, 127n.61, 130n.101, 132nn.129, 130, 131, 132, 133, 133n.147, 134n.158
walnut 113
Wan'an Mountain 123
Wang Anshi 138n.221
Wang Gongchen 138n.215
Wang Kangju 127n.56
Wang Meng 8, 134n.164
Wang River 17
Wang Shiheng 39, 125n.26, 130n.97
Wang Wei 17, 19, 45, 57, 124n.5, 126n.44, 127n.68, 128n.79
Wang Xizhi 133n.156, 137n.208
Wang Zhihuan 128n.82
Wang Zijin 128n.72
Wang Ziyou 137n.208
Wangchuan Estate (Villa) 17, 124n.5, 126n.44
Wanli Emperor 125n.21
Warden Tao 14, 56, 126n.54, 128n.76
Warring States period 124n.3, 129n.88
water 8, 17, 19, 20, 22, 23, 31, 33, 35, 46, 47, 48, 51, 52, 53, 54, 55, 57, 59, 60, 61, 63, 65, 70, 71, 93, 96, 101, 106, 107, 109, 110, 111, 112, 113, 115, 117, 119, 120, 122, 123, 129nn.83, 84, 133n.154, 134n.158, 135n.176, 136n.194

water-caltrop 76, 79, 95, 99, 127n.59, 130nn.105, 107
water-chestnut 130n.105
watercourse 48, 49, 52, 122
waterfall 49, 110, 111, 112, 134n.158
"watershed" see rafter, diagonal
Watson, Burton 134n.170
wattle fence 15, 49, 56
"wave" pattern 89, 99, 101, 102
Wei Zhongxian 12, 124n.16
Weiyang (Yangzhou) 135n.187
Wen, Duke of 37
Wen, Khan of 37, 125n.23
Wen, Lord 52, 127n.62
Wen Xuan see Selection of Literature
Wen Zhengming 20, 21, 31, 35, 54
Weng, Wango 17
West Lake 135n.182
whitewash 25, 94, 96, 107, 127n.61, 132n.130
willow 25, 33, 35, 45, 46, 47, 48, 49, 52, 55, 56, 76, 79, 82, 83, 93, 106, 118, 126n.47, 130n.108
Willow Pool 35
window 11, 18, 23, 45, 46, 49, 69, 70, 75, 76, 79, 81, 82, 84, 86, 93, 95, 97, 107, 109, 110, 120, 121, 122, 130nn.101, 108, 111, 131nn.114, 119, 135n.183, 136nn.200, 201
wine 19, 35, 51, 52, 53, 110, 119, 120, 127nn.65, 69, 130n.104, 133n.156, 136nn.197, 204, 137nn.206, 208
winter 46, 119, 120, 126n.36, 133n.153, 134n.170, 136n.203
women's quarters 81
woodland, woods 18, 31, 45, 47, 51, 52, 57, 65, 100, 117, 118, 120, 121, 123, 137n.207
"woven hat" pattern 102, 104, 133n.145
"woven matting" pattern 102, 104
writing-brush 133n.155
Wu 37, 125n.19
Wu Garden 35, 71, 124n.12, 125n.27, 130n.97
Wu, Marquis of see Zhuge Liang
Wu Youyu 37, 39, 125nn.21, 24
Wu Zetian, Empress 121, 137n.213, 138n.218
Wu Zhen 8, 134n.164
Wucheng, Marquis of see Sun Hao
Wudi see Han Wudi
Wufou 9, 14, 31, 33, 35
Wuhu 135n.178
Wujiang County 124n.13
wutong tree 19
Wuxi 38, 54, 134n.164

Xi Yu 127n.59
Xi'an see Chang'an
Xian Mountain see Da Xian Mountain
Xiang Changping 35
Xiang Rivers 128n.79
Xiang Yu 135n.185
Xiangyang 128n.79
Xiaolinghe 136n.192
Xiaoman 46, 126n.47
Xiaoxia Bay 112, 126n.45
xie 23, 60, 70, 125n.33
Xie He 26
Xie Lingyun 48, 126n.54, 127n.66
Xie Tiao 53, 127n.66
Xi Jia Pond 52
Xining era 122
Xinjiang 128n.73
Xiu Xiu Pavilion 70, 129n.93
Xu Wei 6
xuan 70, 129n.95
xuan rocks 114
Xuancheng County 135n.178
Xuanyuan Mountain 123

Yama 133n.151
yan see penthouse
Yan Hui see Yan, Master
Yan, Master 122, 138n.216
Yan, Stream of 120, 137n.208
Yan Ziyuan see Yan, Master
yang 22, 26, 101
Yang Xiong 129n.85
Yang Ziyun see Yang Xiong
Yangtze River 19, 39, 113, 116, 125nn.19, 25, 135n.181
Yangzhou 20, 21, 42, 45, 54, 67, 72, 92, 115, 124n.9, 135n.187
Yangzhou Yuanlin (Gardens of Yangzhou) 42, 54, 66, 70, 72
Yanshi County 128n.72
Yaofengshan 116
Yellow Emperor 124n.6
Yellow River 128n.82
Yellow, the 53, 128n.70
Yi Jing see Book of Changes
Yi Yu Xuan see Gallery of Seemly Rain
Yi Yuan 53, 59, 63, 75, 100, 119
Yizheng County 124nn.9, 12, 125n.27, 130n.97
yin 22, 26, 101
ying rocks 115
Yingde County see Yingzhou
Yinghu 65
Yingzhou 115, 135n.184
Yixing 113, 116, 134n.170
Yongsheng Street 54
Younger Li 45
yu hua shi see rain flower pebbles
Yu Lin see Forest of Tales
Yu, Lord 56
Yu Sheng 128n.77
Yu's Peak see Southern Peak
Yuan An 137n.207
Yuan dynasty (Mongol) 8, 19, 37, 125n.23, 126n.41, 134n.164
Yuan Ye see Craft of Gardens
Yuling 31

zhai see chapel
Zhan Yuan 22, 46, 51, 76
Zhang Daoling 134n.170
Zhang Jiuling 128n.77
Zhang Liang 115, 135n.185
Zhang, Master 113, 134n.170
Zhang Zifang see Zhang Liang
Zhao Shixiong 137n.207
Zhejiang (province) 12, 125n.25, 130n.105, 133n.156, 137n.208
Zheng Yuanxun 11, 14, 31, 33, 124n.9
Zhenjiang 37, 43, 66, 69, 71, 97, 114, 116, 117, 119, 125n.19, 130n.98, 135n.177
Zhenyang County 115
zhi see angelica anomala
Zhongshan Gate 134n.172
Zhou dynasty 124n.8, 128n.72, 129n.88, 90
Zhou Li see Rites of Zhou
Zhu Sansong 53
Zhuang, Master 60, 129n.83
Zhuang Zi 124n.11, 129n.83, 134n.170
Zhuge Liang 121, 137n.213
Zijin 55, 128n.72
Zijiu 112, 126n.41, 134n.164
Zi Zhi Tong Jian see Comprehensive Mirror to Aid in Government
Zunxian District 122
Zuo Chronicle, The 67, 129n.88
Zuo Qiuming 129n.88